Collective Actions

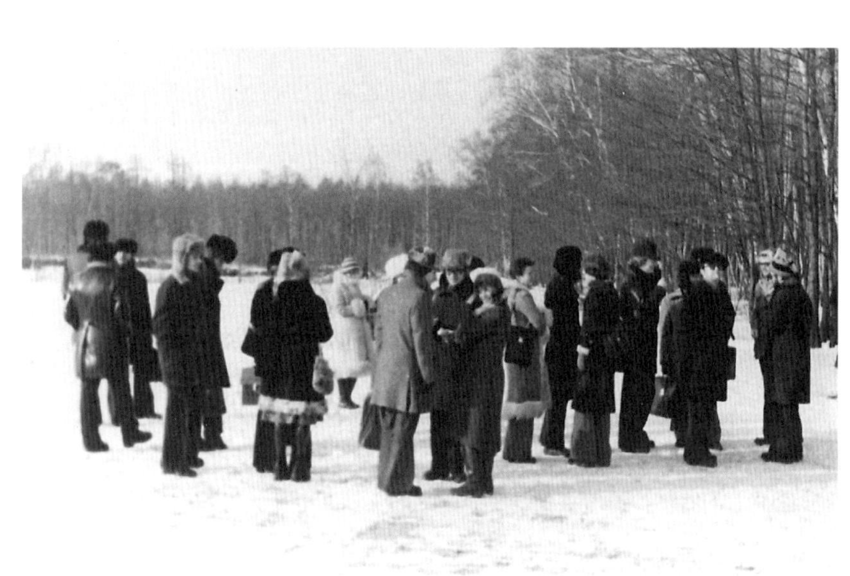

Collective Actions:

AUDIENCE RECOLLECTIONS FROM THE FIRST FIVE YEARS, 1976–1981

Translated and edited by Yelena Kalinsky

Soberscove Press

Chicago

Soberscove Press
1055 N Wolcott, 2F
Chicago, IL 60622 USA
www.soberscovepress.com

Collective Actions: Audience Recollections from the First Five Years, 1976–1981 © 2012 Soberscove Press

Images and Texts (Audience Recollections, Action Descriptions, and Preface from *Trips out of Town,* Vol. 1) © 2012 Andrei Monastyrski and Collective Actions

Introduction, Translator's Note, and English Translations (Audience Recollections, Action Descriptions, and Preface from *Trips out of Town,* Vol. 1) © 2012 Yelena Kalinsky

Library of Congress Control Number: 2001012345
Collective Actions: Audience Recollections from the First Five Years, 1976–1981 /
Translated and Edited by Yelena Kalinsky.

First Printing, 2012

Design by Rita Lascaro
Printed in Iceland by Oddi Printing

ISBN: 978-0-9824090-5-3

Table of Contents

Introduction

Dive-Suits of Factography:
Audience Recollections as Documentary and Action Genre
Yelena Kalinsky

Most of the actions described here consist of a situation in which a group of people is invited by the action's organizers to participate in an activity that is not known to them.[1]

ONE SPRING DAY IN 1976, a pair of poets, an artist, and a student of languages invited a group of thirty acquaintances and friends to a field on the outskirts of Moscow to witness something called *Appearance*. As they rode the commuter train out of the city, the audience members knew nothing of what they were about to see. They were met at the station by one of the organizers of *Appearance* and were led to a snow-covered field, bordered on all sides by a forest, where, two years earlier, after much controversy, the Soviet Union's first uninterrupted outdoor exhibition of underground art had taken place to overwhelming crowds. This time, the field was empty. The audience assembled by the forest's edge and waited. After several minutes, two figures appeared from the opposite side of the field and began to walk in the direction of the audience. Upon reaching the viewers, the pair distributed typewritten "Documentary Certificates," attesting each viewer's presence as a witness to *Appearance*.

Appearance was the first of many durational, participatory actions staged by Collective Actions, a group of performance artists active in Moscow since 1976. Over the years, in particular from the 1970s to the 1980s, these actions played an important role in the development of performance art in the Soviet Union. In carrying out the actions, the organizers and participants explored the nature of the aesthetic event, its relationship to other kinds of performative acts (including poetry readings, avant-garde music, Zen-Buddhist meditation, and Russian Orthodox ascetic ritual), and the fine boundary between

1. Collective Actions, Preface to the first volume of *Trips out of Town*, April 1980. The English translation of this text can be found on page 102 of this book.

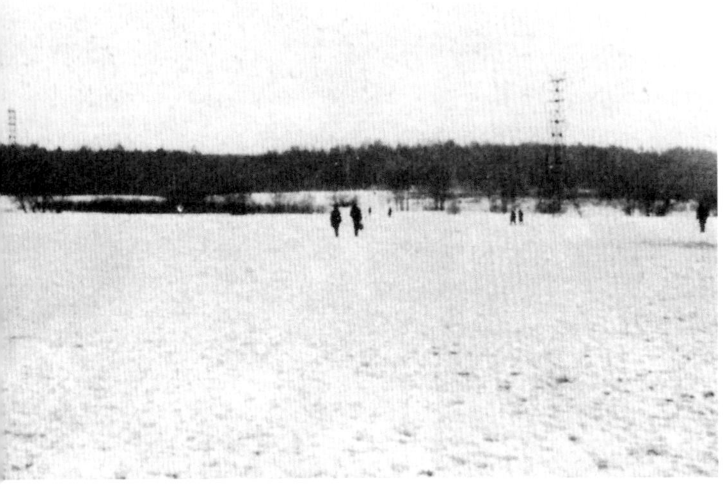

Fig. 1

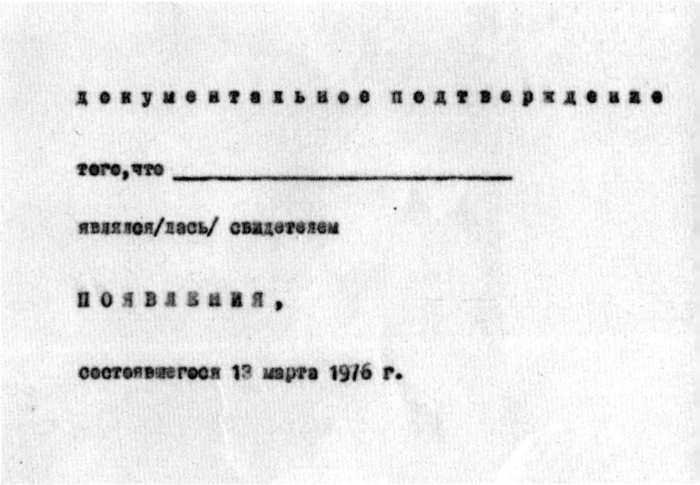

документальное подтверждение

того, что ___________________

являлся/лась/ свидетелем

ПОЯВЛЕНИЯ,

состоявшегося 13 марта 1976 г.

Fig. 2

it and the practice of everyday life. As illustrated by both *Appearance* and the second action, *Lieblich,* in which viewers discovered the sound of a ringing bell buried under snow, Collective Actions' early pieces consisted of minimal action structures performed in nature, far from the urban spaces of the Soviet capital. Often, the actions were followed by lengthy discussions, and this parallel development of formal and theoretical vocabularies about the nature of aesthetic action and experience became one key site of elaboration for the literary artistic movement known as Moscow Conceptualism.

Appearance was organized by Andrei Monastyrski, Lev Rubinstein, Nikita Alekseev, and George Kiesewalter. Monastyrski, Alekseev, and Kiesewalter were soon joined by Nikolai Panitkov, later by Elena Elagina, Igor Makarevich, and Sergei Romashko, and later still by Sabine Hänsgen.[2] The arrival in 1979 of Elagina and Makarevich, whose work within the official Soviet art system gave them access to hard-to-come-by photographic equipment and materials and multiplied the group's ability to document their actions. Makarevich's studio—another rarity for artists—soon came to house a whole series of action-related events, including slide-shows, video

2. Rubinstein did not participate as an organizer after *Appearance.*

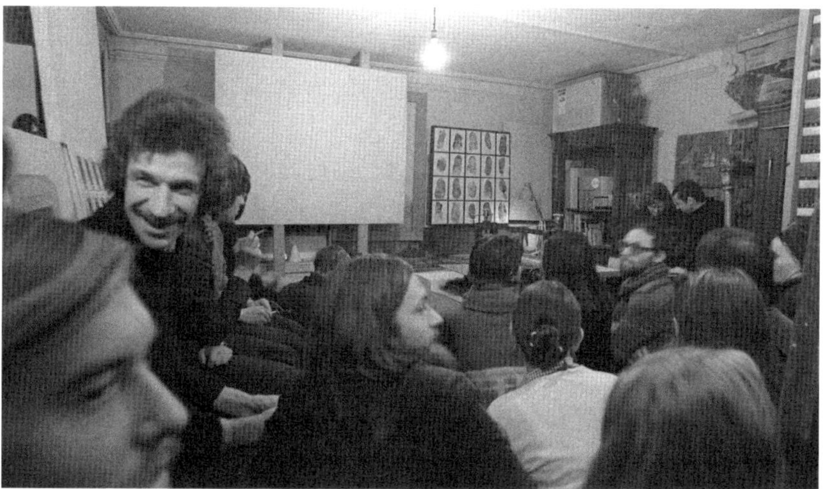

Fig. 3

screenings, and displays of documentary photographs taken during actions, all of which served as catalysts for additional group discussions.

In 1979, Andrei Monastyrski had the idea of compiling a volume of documentary materials related to the group's activities. (Twelve actions had been carried out by then.) *Trips out of Town* came out in the fall of 1980 as a volume of typewritten texts, hand-bound with a flower-printed cloth cover in an edition of four.[3] It contained descriptions of group actions, documentary photographs, a section of members' individual actions, a series of interpretive texts, and a collectively composed preface, which served as a programmatic introduction to the group's activities. Also included in *Trips out of Town* were audience recollections, written upon Monastyrski's request, of eight of the actions in the volume. In attempting to capture the actions from every possible angle, *Trips out of Town* served as a proxy for viewers who had not been present at the events themselves. By aspiring to such total representation, however, the volume seemed to suggest equivalence between the experience of being present at an action and obtaining an image of it as an "anonymous viewer" of documentary material. In his response to

3. For Collective Actions' publication history and location of texts cited in this introduction, see the Bibliographical Note on page 111.

the collective preface, Nikita Alekseev expressed doubt about the possibility of such an equivalence, worrying that the volume might become a "gravestone monument" to the group's activities and an "artificial crystallization" of a still-living practice.[4] Alekseev's concerns turned out to be well founded, though the consequences of *Trips out of Town* and Collective Actions' intensifying documentary impulse did not, in the end, bear out his predictions. Rather than stifle actions, Monastyrski and the remaining members of the group expanded their production of so-called factographic documents, resulting in a redoubled search for ever-newer interpretive frameworks through which to make sense of their evolving practice.

The idea of soliciting audience responses to actions came soon after *Place of Action* (October 7, 1979), a complex work in which each viewer was invited to cross a large, empty field, stopping at pre-determined points along the way to be photographed by a camera located at the starting line. At the end of the action, viewers found themselves in a forested area at the far end of the field, where organizers waited with a tape recorder, and a large signboard hanging on a tree illustrated the complex schema of the various positions of the cameras and viewers during the action. This sudden

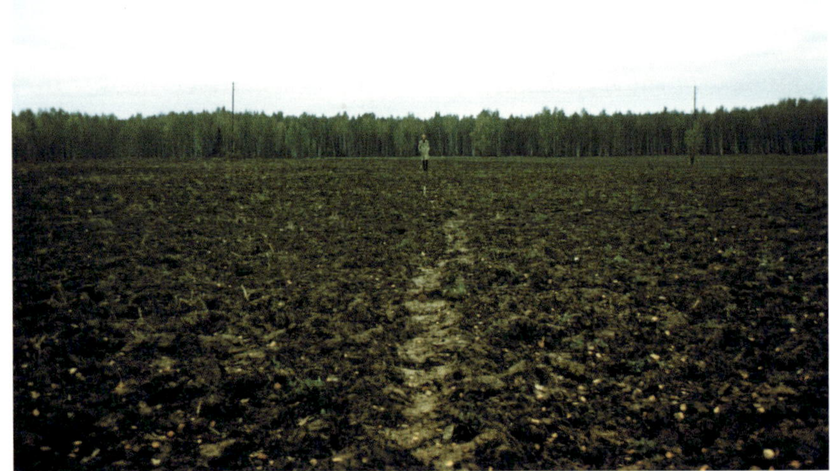

Fig. 4

4. Nikita Alekseev, "On Collective and Individual Actions of 1976–1980" (Aug.–Sept. 1980), in *Trips out of Town*, Vol. 1.

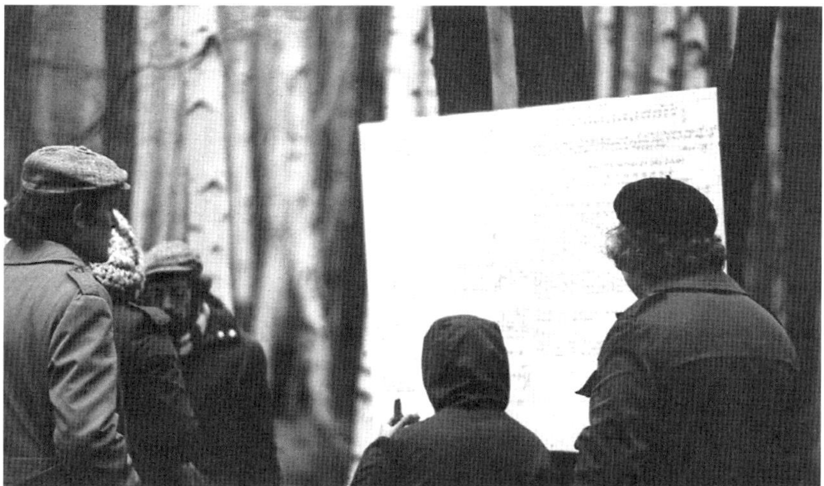

Fig. 5

eruption of documentation, both in volume and variety of media, as well as the impulse to organize, systematize, and sum up a complex set of events through maps, schemas, and extensive group discussions marked a turning point for the group's practice. Monastyrski recalls that it was after *Place of Action* that Ilya Kabakov brought up the idea of collecting audience recollections by soliciting viewer-participants' written impressions, "so that we don't forget."[5] Throughout the following year, with the compilation of *Trips out of Town* in mind, Monastyrski invited several of Collective Actions' regular viewers to record their recollections of actions they had seen. No special instructions were given, and viewers were free to write about any aspect of the actions they liked. Between April and November 1980, six stories about eight different actions were collected for the first volume of *Trips out of Town*: two from Kabakov and one each from children's book author-illustrator Irina Pivovarova, painter Ivan Chuikov, artist Vladimir Mironenko, and Collective Actions member George Kiesewalter. All but Kiesewalter's recollection were written between several months and several years after the actions they describe, and each writer deals in his or her own way with

5. Andrei Monastyrski, correspondence with the author, June 3, 2012.

the problem of recollection, how much and what can be remembered, and what can be conveyed textually of an essentially psychological experience of a spatio-temporal action.

In the context of *Trips out of Town*, the audience recollections are a unique documentary form alongside photography and other kinds of signed and unsigned texts. Photographs, as indexical traces of actual events, have a high degree of documentary veracity. But limited as they are to the brief instant and the photographic frame, they are also fragmentary and selective. Action descriptions, on the other hand, which occupy a prominent place in *Trips out of Town*, strive to be objective, narrative texts that endeavor to capture the structure of each action according to the organizers' original intentions. This systematicity, however, comes at the expense of specific details, unintended outcomes, and personal observations that may have seemed too subjective or irrelevant for the purposes of capturing an action's structure. Audience recollections cut across the different documentary modes of photographs and textual descriptions by providing both a vivid, first-person account of experience and seeking to make sense of the event by means of an interpretive framework, albeit a personal one. In practice, the audience recollections were both an important primary source for the volume's preface and a window into aspects of viewer experience that fall outside the preface's programmatic considerations. Each viewer's story has its own tone and approach to the experienced action, and different viewers' own artistic or philosophical preoccupations often find their way into the viewers' understanding of what has taken place. Ivan Chuikov, for example, whose own work explores the tension between pictorial illusion and paintings as real objects in the world, sees *Time of Action* and *Pictures* as actions that create a particular kind of illusion that gives the audience a chance to experience a revelation and to witness a miracle. Pivovarova, for her part, takes the interminable pulling of the rope in *Time of Action* as an allegory about the temporal experience of contemporary urban life.

Despite the preoccupations of the individual writers, the audience recollections gathered in Collective Actions' first five years (1976–81) share many common themes. One of the most frequently repeated impressions is of encountering something unexpected, being given a gift, receiving a revelation, or witnessing a miracle. In the preface to *Trips out of Town*, the authors explain this aspect of viewer experience as something achieved by giving viewers as little preliminary information as possible and thereby increasing the audience members' anticipation on their journeys to the place of action. Some viewers describe an intense anxiety that they are being tricked or that their commitment in the form of traveling to the place of action—often in poor weather or through deep snow—would be repaid with mockery or derision. But nothing of the sort transpires. As Kabakov writes, "nobody boxed you in the ear, stuffed shit down your collar, or tripped you with a stick."[6] On the contrary, viewers describe how the very minimal movement of figures in the distance, the sound of a ringing bell buried under snow, or the slip of paper on the end of a string pulled across a field were perceived in a heightened state of attention and anticipation as unusual, significant, and having been prepared expressly for them. One of the group's few criteria that determined whether an action would be carried out or not was that the organizers could not predict its outcome, how the viewers would experience the event. The recent emergence of the action genre among unofficial Moscow artists in the 1970s contributed to this sense of unexpectedness, commitment, and payoff so palpable in the audience recollections.

Another theme that emerges in a number of viewer recollections from this period is the fluctuating sense of individual action and collective engagement. Both Kabakov and Mironenko note, with nearly anthropological precision, this shift in the structure of *Place of Action*, in which viewers began as part of a group, gradually separated from it in their passage across the field, found themselves completely alone in a ditch at the culmination of the action, and then rejoined a group of other "initiates" in the forest on the other side of the field. A similar dynamic of separation and reunion figures in Kabakov's description of *Ten Appearances*, where he describes his elation at not having been deceived driving him to rush back to the field to thank the organizers for their gift and to share his impressions

6. Kabakov's Story: *Ten Appearances*. See page 63.

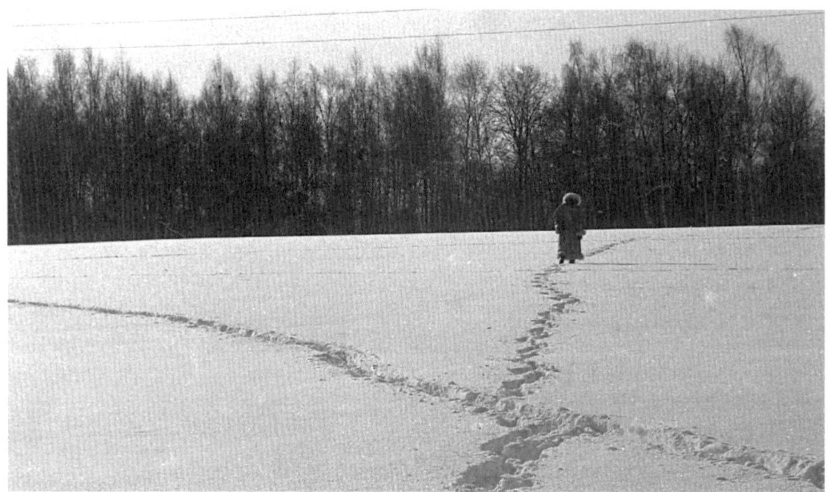

Fig. 6

with the other viewers. Of the same action, Vsevolod Nekrasov writes of his internal resistance against returning to the field, despite having made plans with some of the other participants, feeling that the formal integrity of the action would have been spoiled by a return trajectory and such mundane considerations. Instead, his account focuses on following the natural unfolding of the action, like a centrifugal force, casting him from the center of the field outward and away from the place of action in a powerful gestalt. At the same time, for Pivovarova, the prosaic rituals of strolling in a park, exchanging pleasantries with friends, and watching the children's horseplay in the field during an action were in no way antithetical to the event and feature prominently in her account of *Lieblich* and *Time of Action*. It is notable that experiences of both togetherness and isolation appear in Collective Actions' own theorization of their practice: Nekrasov, Kabakov, and Mironenko's observations of feeling alternatively together and alone at various points in the action are echoed in the group's theoretical texts through the language of subject-object relations, what Monastyrski calls the "dumbbell schema."[7] Likewise, Pivovarova's poetic descriptions of the

7. See, for example, the preface to the second volume of *Trips out of Town*.

landscape, of seeing friends, and of spending a day in the country are precisely the background of the everyday against which Collective Actions sought to locate the aesthetic event.[8]

Prior to *Place of Action* and the compilation of *Trips out of Town* the following year, the term factography, like many others in Collective Actions' emerging critical discourse, was not yet fixed. For Monastyrski, the notion of *factography* was tied to an object or document's having been present at an action, as, for example, the Documentary Certificate in *Appearance*, a piece of rope in *Time of Action*, or the multicolored square constructions distributed at the conclusion of *Pictures*. This definition also included objects left behind, such as the ringing bell in *Lieblich* or the slogan in *For Kiesewalter*, since these, according to Monastyrski, "continued to act for some time after the participants' contact with them during their creation."[9] As such, these "documents" occupied one extreme on a spectrum of documentary modes, which ranged from the indexical to the impressionistic and included, among other things, invitations, photographs, descriptive texts, and audience recollections. The factographic document, for Monastyrski, seems both to have an evidentiary function and to serve as a means of prolonging the experience of action after its temporal conclusion. For Alekseev, on the other hand, the factographic document had a different meaning, which ran counter to that of providing evidence or prolonging action. In his response to Monastyrski, Alekseev offered a more restrictive definition of the factographic document as an element of the action structure that itself played a constructive role in the action's unfolding, such as the Documentary Certificates or the colored envelope constructions from *Pictures*.[10] If factographic documents were to prolong the ephemeral action in some way, Alekseev did not believe that their mere presence at the action, like the magical working of a contact relic, was sufficient. Instead, Alekseev expresses skepticism that an action can exist outside the viewers' spatio-temporal experience of it.[11] In this dispute over terminology, we see already the seeds of two different approaches to documentation that would be taken up by Monastyrski and Alekseev in

8. On this point, see Monastyrski's monologue in his video *Conversation with a Lamp* (1985).

9. Monastyrski defines factography and lists the different forms of documentation used in actions in his "Brief Commentary on Actions from 1976–1979" (June 26, 1979), an early text circulated among group members but not included in *Trips out of Town*. This text was republished in the 2011 Vologda edition of *Trips out of Town.*, Vol.1. (See the Bibliographical Note at the end of this book.)

10. See Nikita Alekseev's "Commentary to A. Monastyrski's Brief Commentary" (July 11, 1979), also reprinted in the 2011 Vologda edition.

11. In his response to Monastyrski, Alekseev writes, "this givenness [of action] is experienced every time anew, and only in this way is it available to perception."

the following years, as *Trips out of Town* was taking shape. Later that year, when the amount of documentation ballooned with *Place of Action*, their difference of opinion began to extend to each writer's understanding of action as such.

In an April 2007 essay, "Dive-Suits of Factography," Monastyrski articulates another definition of factography that had emerged in the wake of Collective Actions' growing documentary impulse in the early 1980s. Reflect-ing on three decades of the group's activities, he writes:

> After the first volume of *Trips out of Town*, practically the entire "spatial-event" and existential horizon of Collective Actions was completely covered over with texts, tracks, marks, and the like. All our creative activity starting some-where in 1981 consisted of work in two directions: on the one hand, toward an even more intensive layering of these traces and texts, and on the other, attempts to break holes through these layers (with each action serving as precisely such an attempt).[12]

In light of the increasingly textual and intertextual nature of subsequent actions, the distinctive character of the early field actions becomes appar-ent. As ephemeral events unfolding in real time and space, the field actions drew their significance from the perceptions of participants who had been there to witness them. "In the actions prior to *Ten Appearances* and *Playback*," Monastyrski continues,

> the events unfolded on an actual out-of-town field (or fields). After these two actions, the fields instead became photographs of out-of-town fields, and we seem to have separated ourselves from reality by a factographic mem-brane. We became clothed in dive-suits of factography, and in them, we maneuvered in the subsequent actions.[13]

12. Andrei Monastyrski, "Dive-Suits of Factography (A General Preface to Three Volumes of *Trips out of Town*)" (April 2007), reprinted in the 2011 volume of *Trips out of Town*, Vols. 6–11.

13. Ibid. *Ten Appearances* (February 1, 1981) and *Playback* (March 1, 1981) were the first two actions of the second volume of *Trips out of Town*.

Here, Monastyrski illustrates the new meaning of factography that emerged in Collective Actions' practice and theory after 1981. It is one that no longer tied itself narrowly to the documentary function, and instead acquired some of the qualities of action in its own right. If Alekseev had worried that an excessive focus on documenting actions would destroy their live qualities, then what Monastyrski suggests instead is a deeper exploration of the very texture of documentation and the discursive spaces of factography. This notion of factography does not function as a means of capturing or prolonging prior actions, but as an event and experience in its own right, one that does not necessarily unfold in real space and time. Like a cosmonaut or a deep-sea diver, the viewer explores its infinitely manifold realms of discourse. Thus, the photographs presented to the eight viewers who returned to the center of the field at the conclusion of *Ten Appearances*—prepared ahead of time to "illustrate" the viewers' reappearances from the forest just minutes earlier—opened up strange new possibilities of experience within the realm of photographic and discursive space. In this way, the spatio-temporal action became but one, material component of the action discourse, a turn that, according to Igor Makarevich, "increased the scope of the action's interpretational field," which now included a variety of performative, documentary, and discursive spaces and dimensions.[14]

The audience recollections translated in the present volume are taken from the first five years of Collective Actions' activities before the period of "factographic discourse," described by Monastyrski. Nevertheless, they might be seen to embody a number of different documentary and factographic modes and thereby span these two very different periods in Collective Actions' practice. The recollections seek to capture the experience of action and at the same time formulate meta-narratives about what has taken place in the field. They create their own discursive spaces through the language of first-person recollection and, as recollections written in the first person, have a pseudo-indexical relationship to the experience of action.

The intention of the present volume is to give English-speaking audiences an entry into audience members' individual, subjective, even at

14. Igor Makarevich, in correspondence with the author, June 6, 2012.

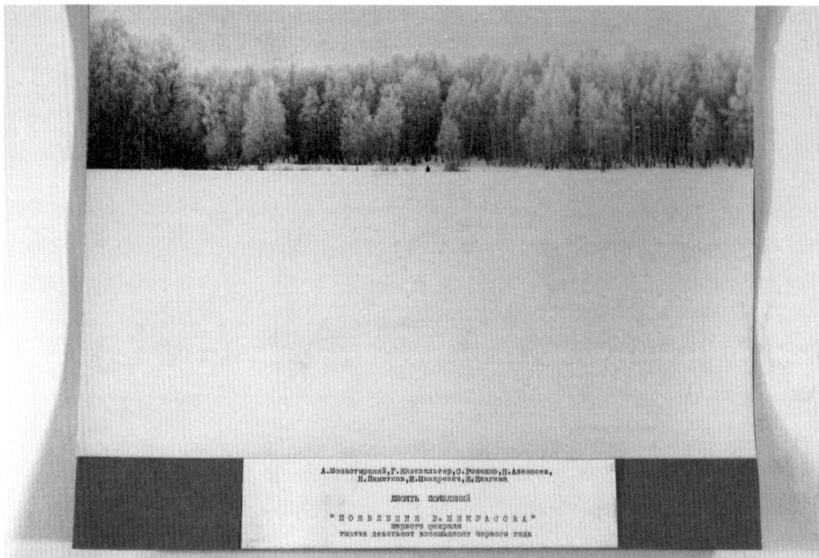

Fig. 7

times eccentric approach to action, one that is rarely glimpsed in Collective Actions' better-known descriptive texts and theoretical writings. This "inside-out" approach to Collective Actions, in which individual experience is given priority over the standardized, "objective" narratives of the other documentary materials, is reflected in the layout of the book itself. Readers are invited to don the dive-suits of factography and explore the hidden contours of action experience through the eyes of the viewers and the lenses of Collective Actions' cameras, and then to pass again through the same actions from another angle, the initial intentions of Collective Actions' authors, whose action descriptions and first programmatic statement are collected in the Action Description section at the back of the book. The hope is that readers will find openings in these many layers, tears in the fabric of the texts, that will serve as invitations to break holes in the perpetual accumulation of time, not necessarily to recapture the past, but to enter into their own subjective experiences of the actions in the present.

Translator's Note

AUDIENCE RECOLLECTIONS convey many shades of meaning through their immediacy and the specificity of their style. At times, they are spoken speech recorded on cassette tape immediately after an action, at others, considered statements about actions that took place months or years earlier. The challenge of translating such texts lies in conveying the particular tone and flavor of each viewer's story. This has occasionally required a fairly loose translation to convey the spirit of a sentence and avoid ensnaring the reader in a thicket of idioms and colloquialisms. Nevertheless, no sections have been cut, and it is hoped that along with the concrete observations about the structure and effects of various actions, what is preserved is the viewers' enthusiasm for participation and eagerness to communicate their experiences. Conversely, in order to preserve the particular pseudo-bureaucratic or pseudo-scientific style used in the action descriptions, the translation has been kept as literal as possible while maintaining a reasonable level of legibility. When ambiguities have crept up in the titles of actions, the more concrete version of the title has been chosen. For example, *Vosproizvedenie* can refer to either the function of a tape player or the mimetic act of replication, and is translated as *Playback* to preserve the more literal meaning. With regard to group members' and audience participants' names, efforts have been made to use the English spelling that each individual has chosen to use, where known. I would like to thank Samantha Fenno and Abe Frank for reading all or part of the text and serving as another pair of eyes (or two); Rita Lascaro for her beautiful layout; Masha Sumnina for prompt and attentive help with the images; Julia Klein for first suggesting that we do this book together and remaining excited about it ever since; and finally, the present or one-time members of Collective Actions: Andrei Monastyrski,

Nikita Alekseev, George Kiesewalter, Nikolai Panitkov, Igor Makarevich, Elena Elagina, Sergei Romashko, and Sabine Hänsgen, for always being generous with their time, their thoughts, their materials, and their friendship.

Yelena Kalinsky
July 2012

Audience Recollections

Pivovarova's Story: *Lieblich, The Lantern, Time of Action*
Irina Pivovarova, November 1980 [15]

The first action that I attended, *Lieblich*, took place about four years ago. We rode to the Izmailovskaia metro station and exited. The park was next to the metro, and there were trees there. We decided to wait for everyone else who was supposed to come. The latecomers were just arriving, and we all soon gathered—I think we were 15 people in all. Although it was early April, it was cold and there was still snow on the ground. This gray, porous snow was melting and it was still quite wintry. Everyone headed to the park, walking for a while along the slushy snow, and soon came to the place where, as though from beneath the ground, from underneath the snow, there emerged a quiet buzzing, something like a ringing bell...I don't know how to put it—there was a sense that some kind of little bell was ringing underground. Everyone began to look at the ground and at each other in surprise. It was apparent that everyone wanted to ask, "What is that?" or to say, "Aha, so this is what we all came here to see!" But just in case, we all continued to look around, wondering if there wasn't anything else that could be connected to this unexpected little bell under the snow. But I don't think there was anything else curious there, just the usual gray sky, the early spring forest, puddles that had melted, alternating with lumpy masses of snow. Everyone looked around at each other, the trees, the sky, and then stood listening to the little bell. Everything was completely casual: some people chatted amongst themselves, some asked about each other's health, the news in Moscow. We stood around this way for some time and then left, and the little bell, I think, continued to ring. Then we all took a

15. The audience recollections have been ordered chronologically according to the dates of the actions they describe, rather than the dates of their writing. The dates of writing are indicated after each author's name.

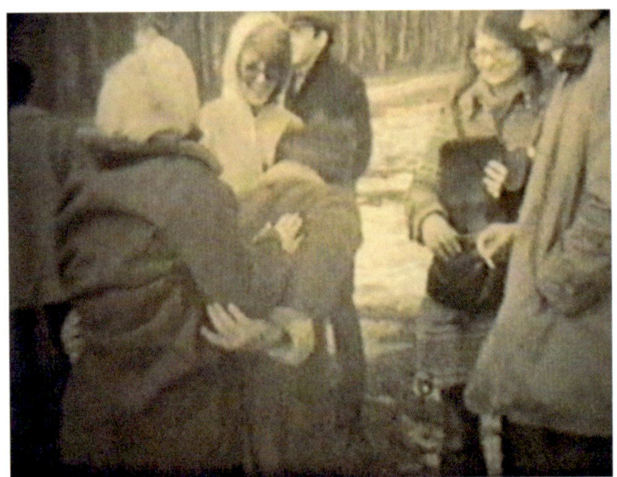

Fig. 8

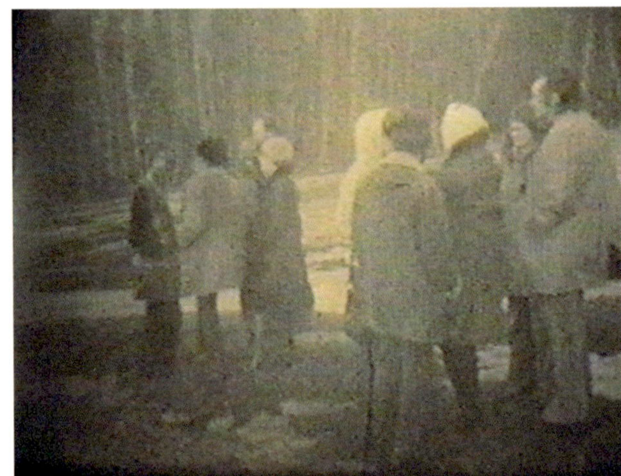

Fig. 9

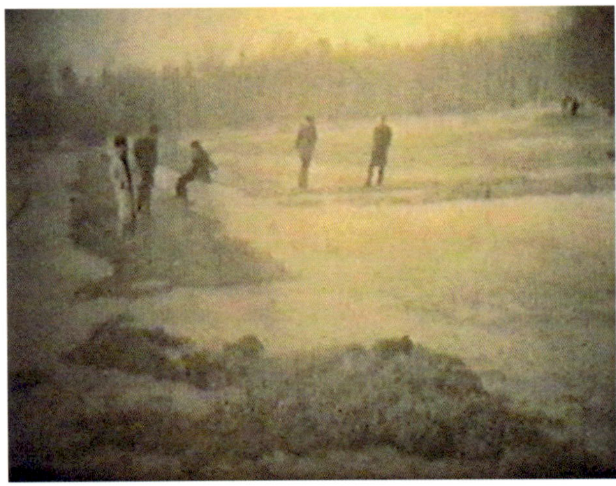

Fig. 10

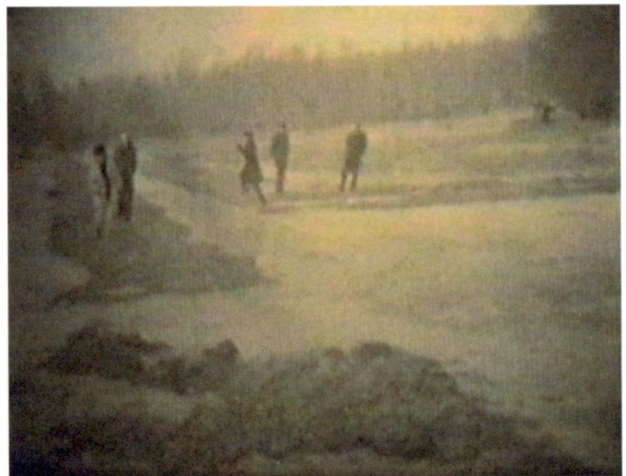

Fig. 11

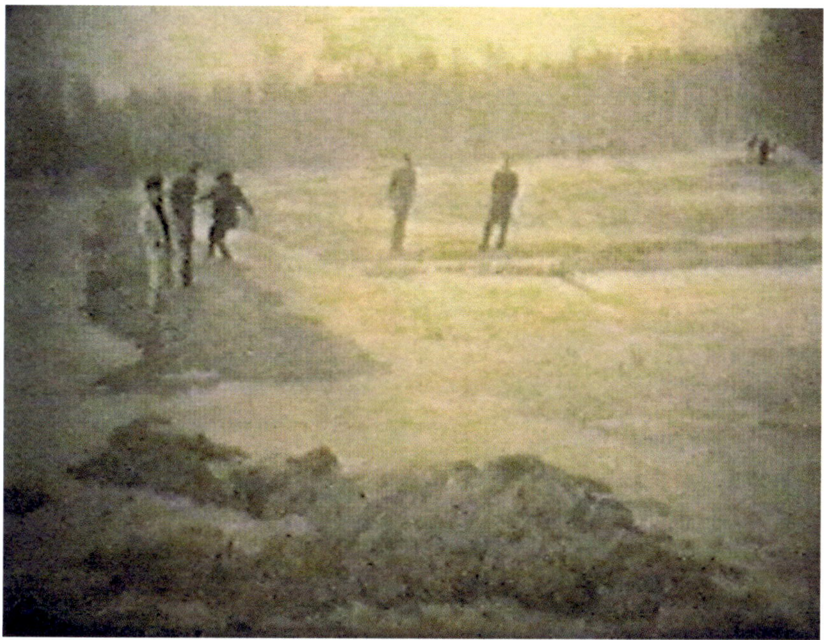

Fig. 12

stroll around the park, and it was very nice. One unexpected experience I remember from this walk was seeing some hearty young men in swim trunks take a dip in the cold pond and rub their giant muscles conspicuously for our amusement.

•   •   •

The second action I attended was called *The Lantern*. This was also a long time ago and so my memories are not very distinct. We rode the Moscow Railway to the Kalistovo station. There were four of us: Nikita Alekseev, Andrei Monastyrski, Igor Yavorsky, and myself.[16] The day was strikingly similar to the one on which *Lieblich* had taken place, although it was the height of winter. The snow was melting, and we also walked through the forest along a narrow little path. It was wonderfully pleasant to walk. I liked the people and had known them a long time. We walked one behind

16. Igor Yavorsky (b.1943), physicist, artist, and regular audience member of Collective Actions' events.

the other, talking along the way. My feet were completely soaked, and Nikita and Andrei each gave me a plastic bag, which I knotted around my feet to make a pair of impromptu galoshes. We came out to a ravine and stopped at the snow-covered slope. Below was either a little river or a half-frozen pond; there were some reeds and some dry, yellowing, half-frozen sedge growing there. After crossing the little bridge to the other side of the ravine, we began to climb the hill. We chose two suitable trees on the slope, and Andrei climbed up one of them and tied the rope to it. Then we threw the rope over to the other tree, tied the lantern to the middle of it, attached a big inflatable toy ball to the lantern, and twisted the rope up tightly. When we let go of this twisted-up lantern, it began to spin and the light began to flicker, flashing very fast around the clearing. The light of the lantern was filtered by a purple glass. It was very pleasant and very fast flickering. It lit the trees up one by one and the spaces between the trees seemed to snatch them out of the darkness, and this impression was intensified by the fact that a very thick and dense dusk quickly descended. We seemed to be watching a film starring the trees, each one different: tall,

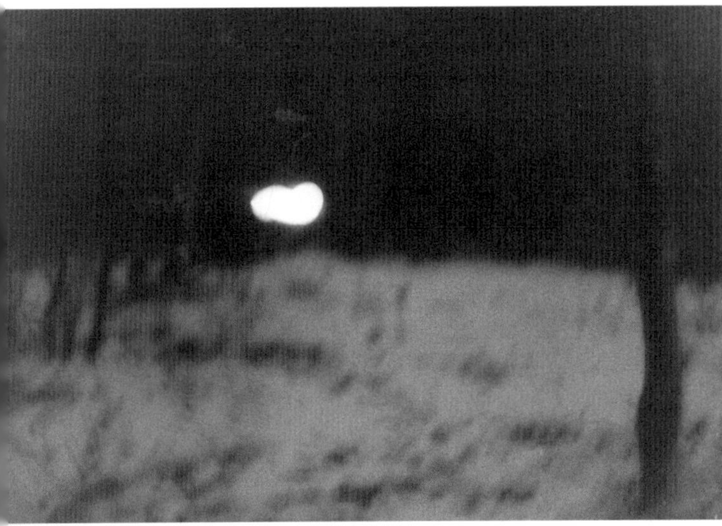

Fig. 13

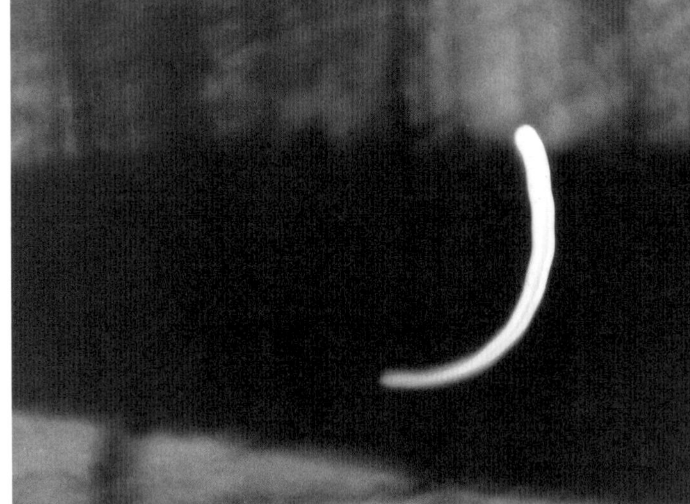

Fig. 14

thin, thick, white, brown, covered in leaves, or bare. It was like a circular panorama of the forest: in the small space around the lantern, one by one, each tree revealed its face and instantly disappeared, and then flickered anew. The ball had been attached to the lantern apparently in order to slow down this flickering, or, perhaps, so that the fairly strong wind could act its part once we left. Without us now, it used the ball to swing the lantern. We watched for some time longer before starting the descent. Retreating, we constantly looked back at this flickering purple light. Then we crossed to the other side of the ravine and stopped. At this point, the snow started to fall, a white snow, falling in the dense twilight. I clearly remember the fast movement of the snow, and behind it, this flickering of the lantern, the flickering of a purple glowing point. It had the appearance of someone standing there making signals, although we knew that there was no one there. And all the same, the place we had just abandoned seemed alive, to operate on its own: that little clearing with the trees and lantern putting on a small surprise for us. It was as though we were witnessing the creativity of that place, of this clearing, of these trees. This was enjoyable, not

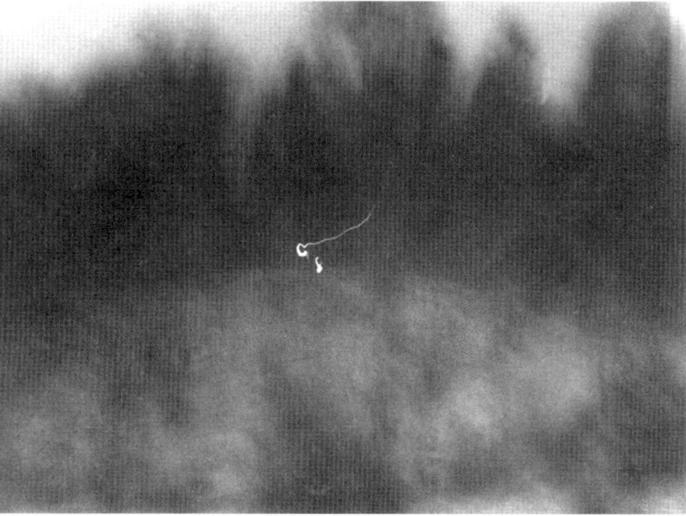

Fig. 15

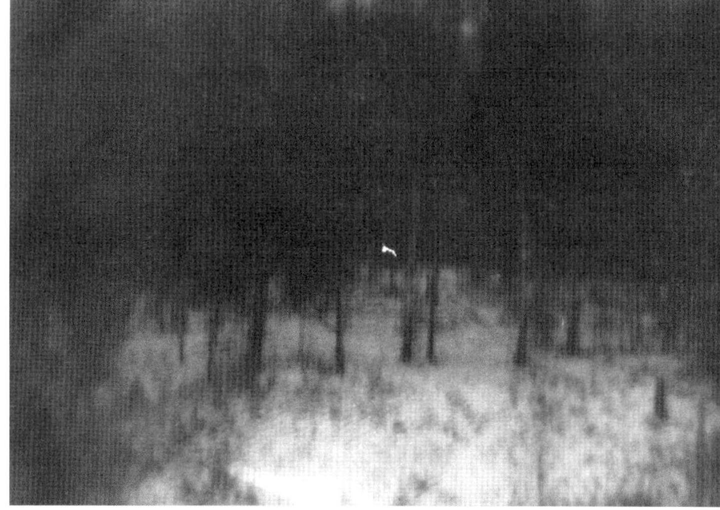

Fig. 16

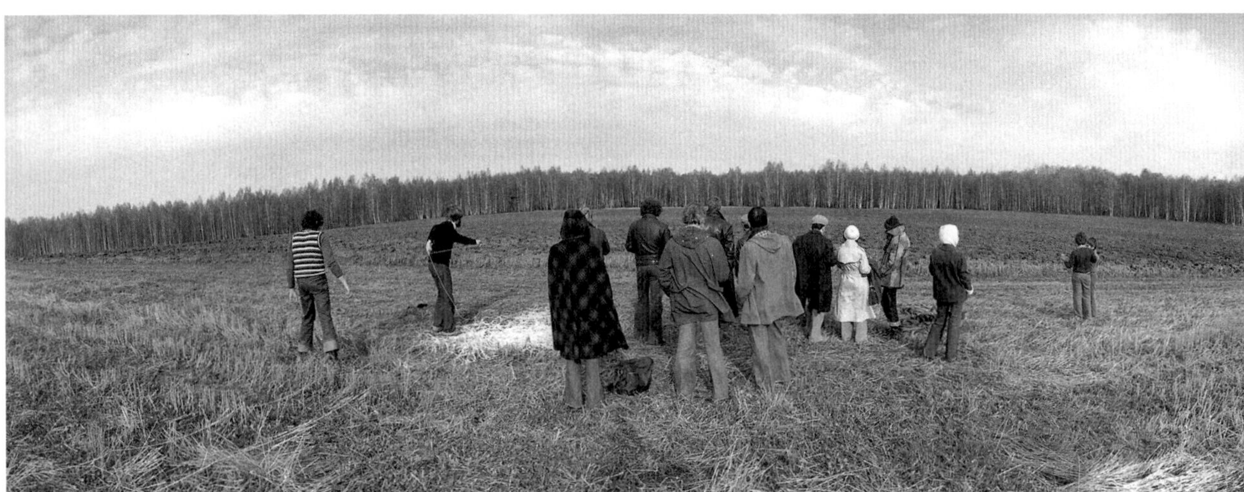

Fig. 17

forced, and calm. We watched with pleasure through the flying snow. And then there was a nice coincidence of different movements. The sheet of snow before us, and farther along, completely far away, an entirely different movement, not corresponding to this one. But all the same, everything had a rhythm, the rhythm of the approaching night, perhaps, or even the rhythm of our mood. Everything was extraordinarily calm, peaceful, and, I would even say, pure. We stood there for some time until it got completely dark, and then we turned and walked through the snow-covered village streets to the station. We no longer looked back, as we would not have seen anything but the roofs and the houses of the village. Instead, we boarded the train and returned to Moscow.

·   ·   ·

The next action at which I was present, *Time of Action*, took place two years ago. This time, the day was completely different, a bright day in the early fall. We rode from the Savelovsky rail terminal to the Lobnya station, boarded a bus, and were on our way. We exited at the stop and walked to a large field, half ploughed and half overgrown with green grass. Apparently, there had been potatoes planted there and these potatoes had been gathered up. Some lone spuds were still lying around; you could see them in the thick black earth. We came up to the edge, where overgrown grass ended and these ploughed-up furrows began, and this is where the action itself began. The clearing was surrounded by forest, and from the other side, the rope stretched out to us along the field, its end lying before us. Somebody, most likely Monastyrski, took it up and started pulling. He pulled and pulled. We stood and waited to see what would happen next. Everyone watched as he pulled the rope, understanding that the action had already begun. But Monastyrski still did not stop pulling. It was taking a very long time. Some of us sat down, some began to walk around and gaze in different directions. Somebody else took up pulling the rope. There was a decent amount of it over on our side already, but the rope still did not end. Then a third person—a gray-haired Moscow artist—began to pull the rope a bit coquettishly. But the rope did not even think about ending. Zigzags of rope fell to the earth and everybody thought: my goodness, but what could this be, what will happen next, how interesting. What if the other end of the rope is tied to a rabbit or, say, a pot of boiled potatoes? But no, nothing of the sort materialized, and instead the endless line of rope continued, which someone reeled in very energetically, in big swinging motions, while someone else reeled like a sailor on a merchant ship. Someone, having replaced the sailor, did it with graceful, flamboyant movements, and then someone else played to the gallery, with antics and theatrical effects. Somebody did it extremely steadily, somebody else very timidly. Those who did not take part in the physical process itself continued to walk around the field and watch. The day was very beautiful. And the rope kept coming and coming. The audience had time to grow hungry. Some took out sandwiches and apples and began to eat. There were children, and they began to get mischievous and fool around. And the rope kept coming, and coming, and coming... It seemed like an hour had gone by, two, but the rope kept coming, and coming, and coming. Then we saw a person walking along the edge of the field gathering potatoes into a sack. This attracted everyone's attention and

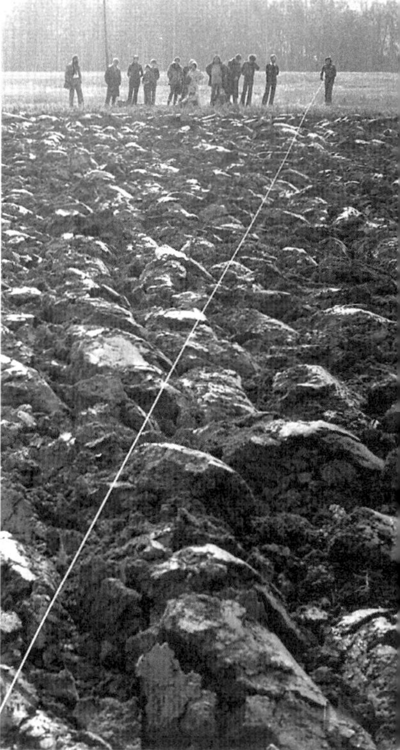

Fig. 18

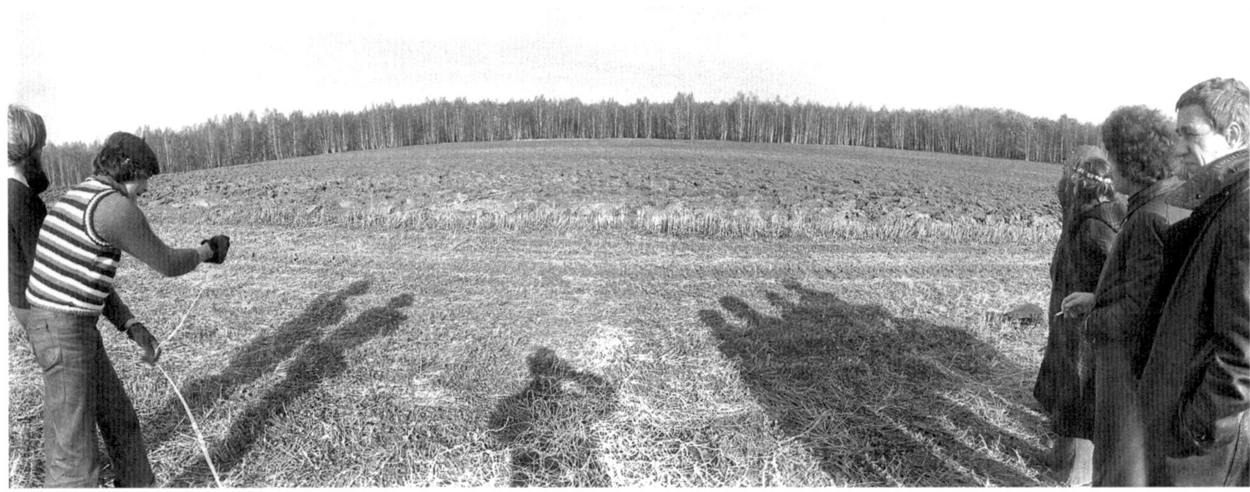

Fig. 19

17. Maria Konstantinova
    (b. 1953), painter, frequent
    participant in actions, and
    then spouse of Collective
    Actions' member Nikita
    Alekseev. She is indicated
    as M.K. in all action
    descriptions.
18. Natalia Shibanova (1948–
    2008), painter and graphic
    artist, and then spouse of
    Collective Actions' member
    Nikolai Panitkov.
19. Nikolai Panitkov (b. 1952),
    artist and founding member
    of Collective Actions.

entertained them, since we had all had time to get a little bored with this never-ending rope, thinking to ourselves, so what? A rope is a rope—very nice, of course, outstanding, fabulous. But the public seemed to be hungry for some new action, some new impression. That is why everyone looked on with much pleasure at this elderly citizen gathering potatoes. We had all had the greedy thought ourselves already: should I gather some potatoes? For a time everyone forgot about the rope and secretly yearned to exercise his domestic tendencies, since I think there were no potatoes in Moscow at the time. And what came next? Next someone, some of the women, I think, Masha,[17] Natasha Shibanova,[18] yes, appeared from the other end of the field, from where the rope was being pulled, and then went back, and I went with them. I wanted very much to see what it was all about, what the trick was. They were leading me there. And there, next to a large tree, stood the very tall Kolya Panitkov[19] beside a drum on which an enormous amount of rope was still wound, a massive amount. I thought, Lord, when will it end? It will probably last until evening. This is, of course, terribly wonderful, very interesting, but nonetheless, a bit unusual for Moscow's bustling, hurried life. We

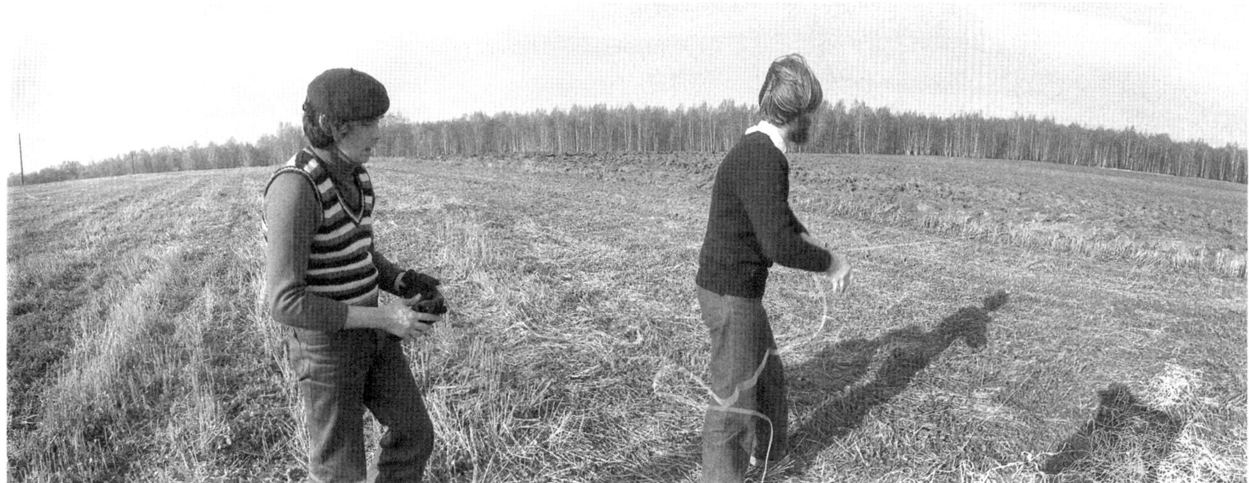

Fig. 20

are people used to guarding every minute, every second. We are perpetually running, perpetually in a hustle and bustle, always hurrying, never having enough time, and here all of a sudden this inexcusable waste of time. How can this be? Time flows so freely, wastes itself on practically anything. At the same time, it was nice to become aware of this. Aware that … and why not? Maybe all of this economizing that we are doing is actually empty. And maybe this very long action is actually time filled up. At any rate, it did not have a sense of emptiness, but of abundance, sufficiency. I cannot explain why there was this sense of abundance. Maybe it was not in the rope itself, but in the lovely fall day in combination with the ploughed field, the potatoes, this rope, in the children running around nearby. Everyone seemed busy with his own task, and the rope still continued to come. Or maybe, somehow, purely subconsciously, the analogy occurred to me that the rope is time, which comes and comes. We are all busy with our own lives, while the rope comes and comes. But all the same, despite its endlessness, sooner or later, it will run out. And that is how it was. Despite its endlessness, it ran out. The drum on which it had been wound was emptied, and on the

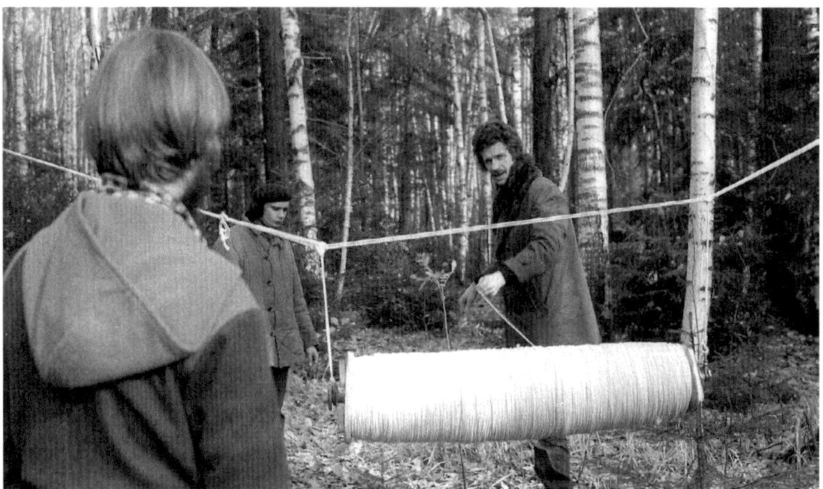

Fig. 21

border between the grass and the black earth lay an enormous pile of rope. Everyone sighed a certain sigh of relief—finally. Though it was not clear why everyone sighed this way. It must be because we each have some reflexive feeling of the necessity of an action's conclusion. The action's span must end with something; we are not used to action all by itself, without a "full stop." And so, the "full stop" arrived in the form of an enormous pile of rope in the field. It is fairly extraordinary, if you think about where this pile came from—it was perfectly impossible. Imagine, once we leave, that citizen or some other lady citizen coming to the field for potatoes and chancing upon this rope. They will be guessing for a long time where such a fine rope had come from. Some thought that we should take it home, but there was so much of it, such a gigantic amount. Then in the end, I think, it was dragged away anyway to the dacha. (Kolya Panitkov had a dacha nearby.) We all went to the dacha, too, and had a very nice time and a few drinks there. The more distant acquaintances left and the closer circle stayed at the dacha. We stayed there until evening, and then in the evening, contented and tired, went home.

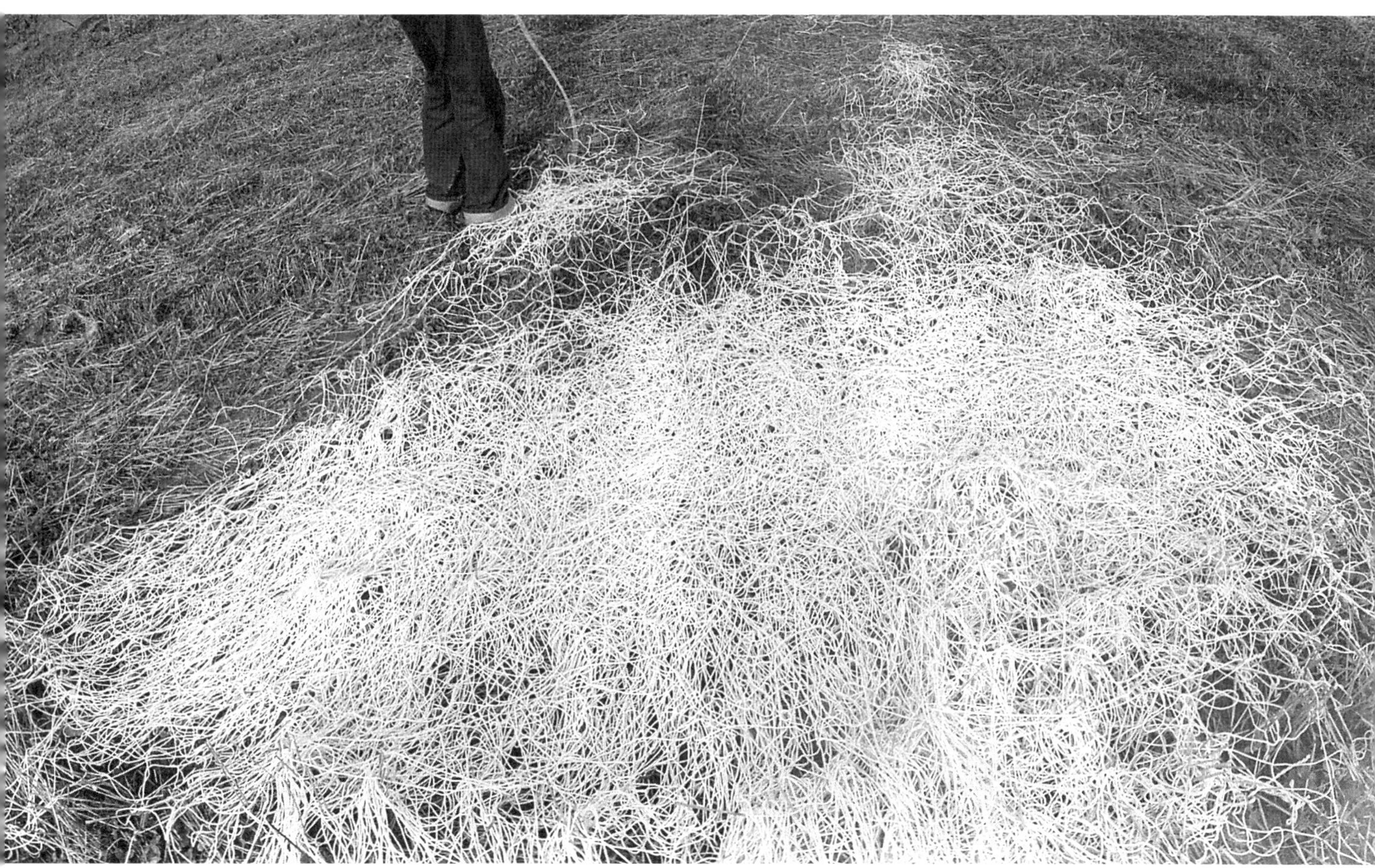

Fig. 22

Kabakov's Story: *Comedy, The Third Variant, Pictures*
Ilya Kabakov, April 1980

Much time has passed by now, and it is interesting to try to think of what it was that you experienced back then. Interesting what the mind has preserved of those long-ago impressions. It seems that what was stored as an experience has remained firmly as a residue. It will not disappear. I am now remembering what I actually remember, and not the things that I would wish to recall or any other secondary details.

The first action that I saw was *Comedy*. It was my first time at such a performance, or rather, event, and the strongest initial impression that I had was of an unexpectedly elevated and pleasantly comfortable state linked to the thought that here we are on our way, and I know for sure that I am not here on a task. This journey is extraordinary because, perhaps for the in my life, it is not taken to complete some task. It is not even taken for a pleasant time, since that too is a kind of task. You are literally cut off and stripped of all forms of individual intention. Here, some truly very comfortable strata of the psyche are liberated, as though you were internally jumping from the feeling of impunity, the feeling of freedom in the most precise sense: a greater freedom than practical or social freedom, or any other kind. Ahead of you lies only that which you cannot even imagine. An interesting vacuum appears. Even when you are called to celebrate and you know for certain that you will not be doing anything but looking around and eating—still, the knowledge of what awaits you already poisons some hidden, unfeeling aspect of your psyche. Whereas here, the fact that first, you are not setting out upon some task, and second, you can in no way predict what is about to happen, produces a euphoric state. The vacuum of this mental space possesses an incredible level of joy, a feeling of being charged up, and a readiness to perceive on the highest of levels. One could call it a kind of pre-sentiment of a miracle, or in any case, a complete readiness for one.

Next I would like to describe our movement through the forest. You find yourself in some kind of double state there. On one hand, you are simply walking in the forest where you have walked for many years, but always, you remember, with some definite and clear intent: to relax, to breathe the air, to see people, in any case, to do something pleasurable. But here, on the other hand, you are clearly going with an uncertainty, and at the same time, in the same forest where you have always strolled. And so, the forest takes on a completely new and unusual character. It seems like the same forest, but it is strangely activated. All of these branches, grasses, and paths through which you strolled so many times. You touch the leaves literally for the first time and are the first to tread on the grass. And this careless-happy and simultaneously terribly sharpened and charged state does not weaken.

Then, finally, you emerge from this amazing forest. There is no fore-thought that you will come out and something will be there, because the effect of the forest is already so unusual and extraordinary. Then we are told that we should stop here. I remember the slight chill, when everyone else had already stopped and I was still walking. I had some kind of sharp pains in my heart telling me they had not deceived me, that precisely here is where it would take place. Such trust in the organizers is remarkable. I had no thoughts that I might be deceived, that some scoundrel might lead me around, but then say: there's the station just over there, and all the while you were wandering around like a fool. No, everything is exactly how you had expected. This moment of un-deception was very important. That you will actually see it now. The experience is incomparable, like you have finally reached this moment—which one precisely does not matter to you, since you find yourself in a state of pre-anticipation of some event, and everything else projects in colorful relief against the background of the event that is about to take place.

And here now is this empty, hump-backed field. It is unusual, entirely colored by your state of pre-anticipation. A curious alliance arises between the people who have come specially: although we did not come here to be shown something, this is exactly what is about to happen, and what's more, it will happen simultaneously in the air, and in the forest, and inside of us. I do not understand where this feeling comes from, this feeling of being called, as it were, to see something. It is a very powerful experience. You get the feeling that the air, the field, all of this is no accident, and everyone is ready for it. You do not feel any prosaicism, artistry, or artificiality, that they have brought you here to show you something, that they've concocted something—ah, yes, let us see what you've come up with—nothing of the sort. There are no stage wings, there is no machinery. You are in complete accord with everything. You understand that the ones who have brought you here and are aware of everything will themselves be similarly surprised. There remains no division between actors who will show and viewers who will watch. There is the sense of a first time and that is this way for all.

It is important that the field is a field of anticipation, that space is a space of anticipation. And the time in which you see nothing but feel it is also sheer anticipation. This, in essence, is the vacuum. This entire state is the vacuum, some kind of extraordinary reservoir, a continuum of anticipation, a cut-out in the space-time of anticipation.

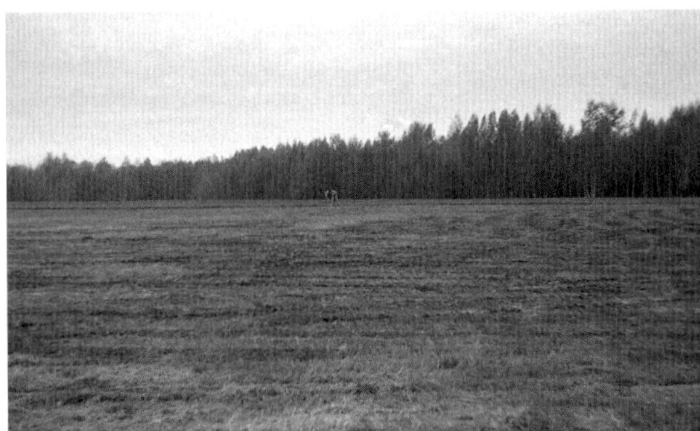

Fig. 23

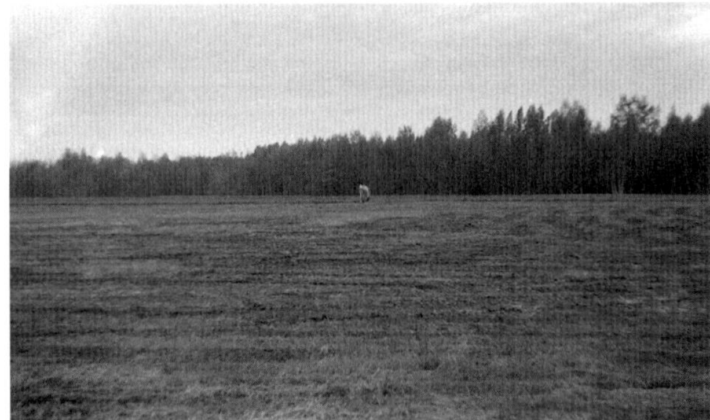

Fig. 24

And then somebody says: *there, there, look, look.* I remember perfectly that there was no one in the field just now, and the next second—an extraordinarily important one when there was nothing there and then it became visible—I saw two flickering points, glimmering and indistinguishable, moving along the field. It was an unusual experience, because everything was taking place at such a distance that it depended entirely on the effort of my looking. I understood that my psyche had linked up with my straining vision. When I strained my eyes, I saw them; when I did not strain, I did not see them. I could look at the tree and so on. I began to feel that this looking was linked to a mental trope, a mental proverb. If you look, you will see; if you do not look, then you will see nothing. It was as though the metaphor had been presented to you to experience. It all depended on your will, on your consciousness. I have to say that I immediately liked this very much. It was not like when people throw themselves before you, but rather, it was your consent, or more accurately, the accommodation of your attention and vision, that was the guarantee and condition of the entire event.

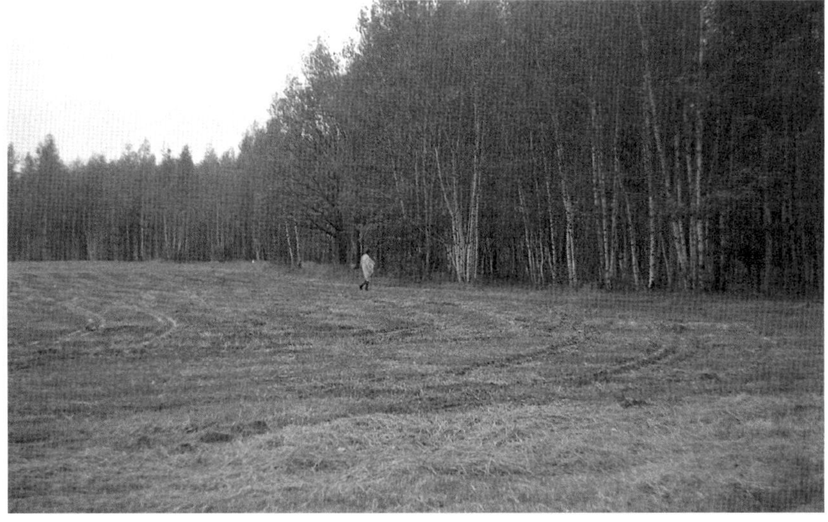

Fig. 25

Then gradually, I assure myself that their movement takes place neither past, nor towards us, but seemingly obliquely. They seem to be approaching, but not quite approaching. This hypotenuse line, or more precisely, a kind of equal measure between movement parallel to us and movement towards us, this too created a strong impression. It is as though the moving figures do not concern themselves with us, but on the other hand, they are interested somehow, since they do after all come nearer. There is a kind of painful and torturous state here: it grows more and more visible, but not so much that it is completely visible; it seems to take place a little bit for us, but not completely for us. And so gradually, but already distinctly, I can make out two moving figures. I must say that no questions—why two figures, what does it mean—came to mind. The strangeness of what was taking place was such that all questions seemed to disappear. The color of the cloak produced a very strong impression. It had to do with the transparency of everything around us. The forest, even with all its strangeness, was transparent. The sky was transparent. Everything was familiar and transparent, except the color of the cloak, which was completely inexplicable. If it had been, for instance, red, then it too would have been transparent. It would have been a person in a costume, a strange one, yes, but this could be ascribed to the event. But here the cloak was painted like the sky, like the forest, like the earth. Its incompleteness, hazy middle, different bottom, and so on, produced a very strong impression—apparently because the inexplicability and improbability of this coloration seemed to redouble easily and blend into the unusualness of the event.

Then finally, the figures stopped. Something was happening out there with them. I figured out the narrative for myself later. But I am now remembering that at the time, I had the feeling that they seemed to be conversing, that it was something incomprehensible, that they seemed to be leading some kind of life out there. Then one of the figures disappeared, and from that moment on, the form of the cloak became rounder—one of the figures had climbed under it. Ah, that's it: it was a kind of reverse or backwards birth, and now it is one large figure moving in this state of "pregnancy." At

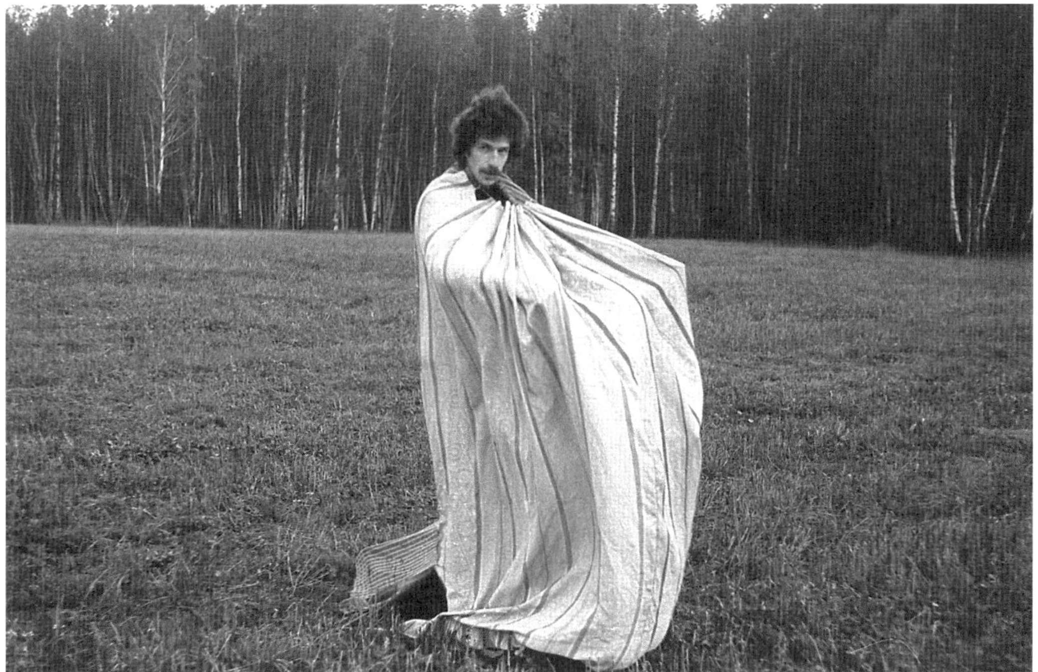

Fig. 26

this point I have some kind of gap in memory. But then suddenly, I remember, the cloak seemed to have been removed, or rather, he lifted it up and carried it under his arm, as if to demonstrate his opened cavity. And there was no one there, there was no one and nothing there. As I remember it . . . where did he . . . a terrible situation. In other words, it was as though he had already given birth and was not even pregnant any longer, as though no longer with child, I cannot remember now, but it leaves this very strong impression of a kind of lost conception. However, as strange as it may seem, I can only describe this moment rationally now. That is, I can only understand it as the reverse of birth, i.e., as a loss. There are these kinds of artificial pregnancies—the stomach grows, but there is nothing there—these psychological anomalies, neuroses.

I did not care at all where he had gone. I had already experienced enough states. Everything else, negating or exposing, I had no interest in. Although I did hear the rather worried voices of the other viewers: where did he disappear to, won't he catch a chill, etc. But this did not interest me at all. I understood the central event, I repeat, as a rational-conceptual one. The subconscious impressions were elsewhere, although the proverb itself produced a strong impression too. Then there was the experience of this person's departure into the bushes at a certain distance from us. I began to distinguish some of his personal characteristics: the trousers, the hands, the movement of the legs, and then the bushes into which he disappeared. He had previously been at such a distance that he was almost indistinguishable. Only his fantastical action was visible, along with nature, with the air, with my frame of mind. And this situation of "nothing special," as if he were to say, *I was just walking here and now I am leaving,* in contrast to that earlier appearance from nonbeing and spatial emptiness, produced once again, as a moment that closes a circuit, a very powerful impression. In other words, it is interesting that the action's center, its contents, turned out to be beyond the threshold of my sensibility. I perceived the action itself rationally, while the arrival, the forest, the appearance of the figures, the anticipation, the slow movement, and the departure seemed extraordinarily dramatic. The event culminated in me, so that I did not even suspect that somebody had remained in the field.

The intense impression of the cloak immediately associated this entire construction with the realm of some kind of magical, Biblical events, and specifically Biblical, not Eastern. I think that at the heart of this action lies the image of "birth."

•   •   •

Now I will say a bit about *The Third Variant.* Since it was now my second time in this forest, there were no new impressions from the journey, but instead repetition of those same experiences. I remember arriving at the same place, just down a way. It was a very nice day.

I remember, somebody very tall walking and then laying down. A certain amount of time passed in waiting. Well, I thought, so he lay down,

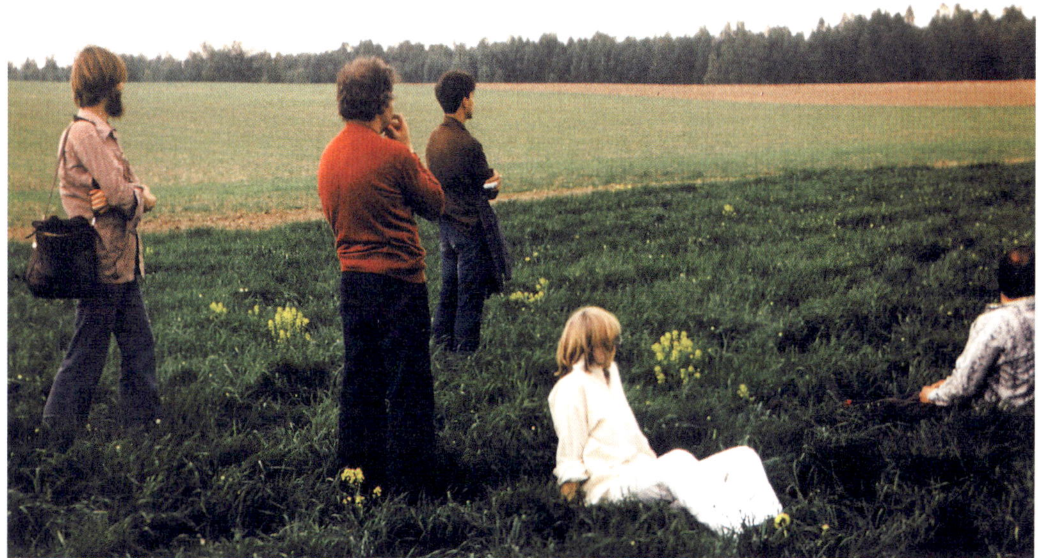

Fig. 27

and what will happen next? And here my waiting ended. At a distance of about thirty meters from where he had lain down, another person stood. In place of a head he had a tear-shaped object, I think it was red. This tear was perched with its sharp end toward the cloak. Then the figure somehow started walking. I must say that I am experiencing some kind of mental discomfort now, even though I followed everything very carefully and liked what was taking place, both that a person walked, lay down, and was no longer there, and that after some time another person rose in the correct place. Curiously, in my memory, this second figure began to walk a tiny bit (though in reality he had not moved). I feel that this is a function of inertia related to the first figure's movement, when he was walking and stopped. Apparently, his kineticism continued to live on in my mind, and for this reason the second figure began to walk ever so slightly. But on the other hand, despite the figures' identical costumes, the realism of the surrounding situation was such that I could not allow that this figure had crawled through some kind of trench, and so it did not seem to me that it was the same figure. And so, the second figure moved and its balloon popped, producing smoke. I must say that this was rather more extravagant than natural. But since everything was taking place in nature and the conditions of the field, the distance, the mysteriousness, the intrigue, etc. had been maintained, this did not seem disharmonious, but instead somehow playful and scandalous. Although the action itself did not end there, artistic completeness was once again realized. My displeasure did not lie in the action as a whole, but in essentially one thing: in the too short temporal distance between the two most important steps, between the lying down of the first figure and the appearance of the second. This distance turned out to be painfully brief. In my opinion, this time should have been stretched out three or four times longer. Because here is the situation: so a figure lay down in a ditch, so what? But at the same time, this creates a pre-anticipation that something should take place. The tension of this thread should have been drawn out right then at the beginning of

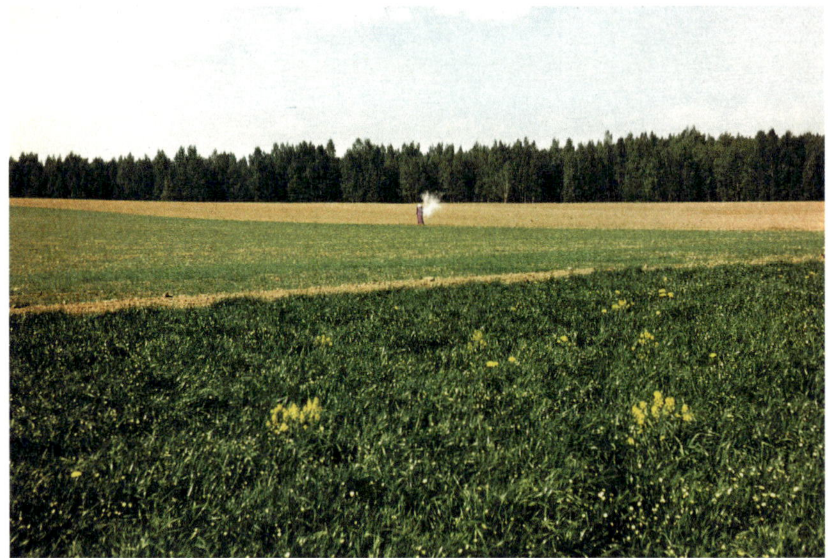

Fig. 28

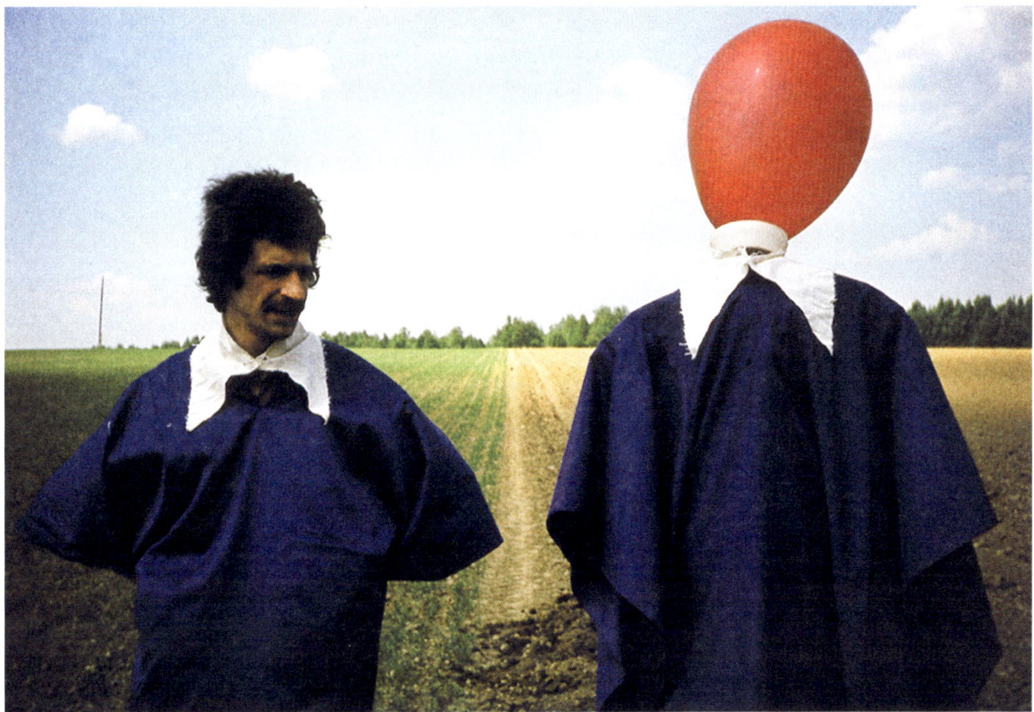

Fig. 29

anticipation . . . In other words, due to the rapid-fire speed, the "empty" time had failed.

The return journey after the action produced the same pleasant feeling as the arrival. The sense that you have not been tricked, that it was something genuine, is preserved and then gradually disappears; here is the swamp, the little bridge, the train platform, the commuter train, and at each step the residue of the event remains. The mental comfort of pre-anticipation is preserved.

• • •

And now regarding the third thing that I saw, which was *Pictures*. This thing produced the best impression, and no questions came to mind. Of the more memorable impressions, I remember that we all had to be doing

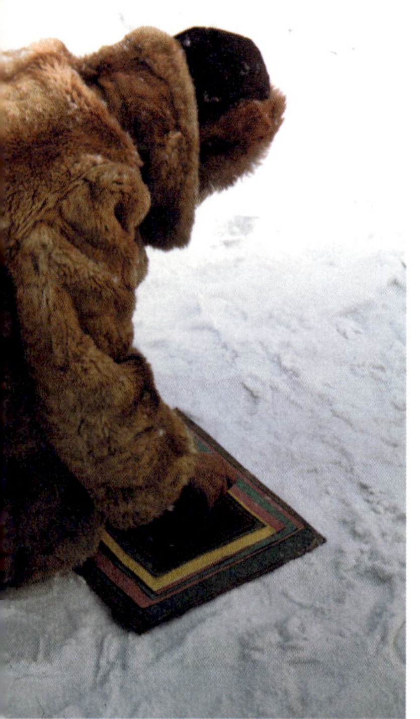

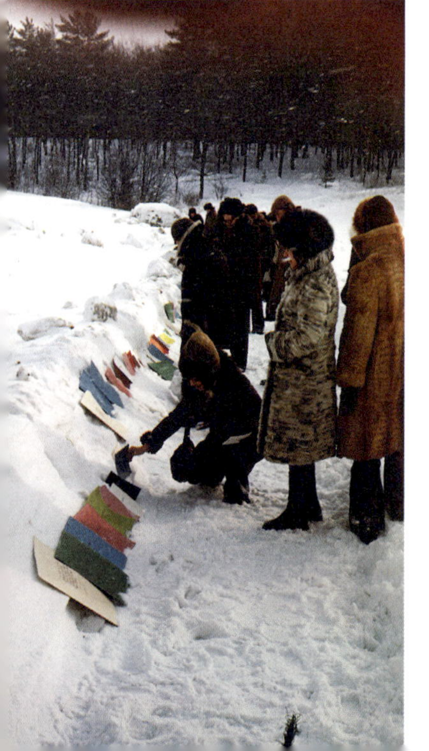

above: Fig. 30; below: Fig. 31

something—but this something was so strange and at the same time so easy and light that it was like one of those trivial jokes that could be easily brought out and was itself easy to follow. Both the instructions and the program itself were simple and not burdened by understanding. That is, the understanding of the maneuvers did not get in the way of the anticipation of what would be taking place, though at this point it was unclear what that would be.

We were placed at equal distances, each a large distance apart, and each busy with his own task. And at the same time, we were all busy with the same nonsense. This very non-communality, non-solidarity, and at the same time, a kind of unity—all of this created a field of freedom.

The writing on the slips of paper matched what we were doing. It was all easy to recognize. What was written was essentially what was taking place—and this produced a very pleasant and positive impression. The text said "winter," and it was winter all around, and there was a kind of pleasure in it, that what was written matched what was taking place. But at the same time, this contrast between what is written and what is taking place is also where things diverged. After all, what is written is nonsense, letters, words, while on the other hand, there is nature, and in coming together, the two things bifurcated one's impressions terribly.

But the most remarkable thing that happened was when all these colored squares were glued together, and we received this kind of block-composite, that is, when we received the object. This is what created the most wonderful impression: all of these words pasted one over the other, never to be disclosed again. It was extraordinary how completely this linked up with the memory of that day and of the entire event. It cannot be repeated, after all, not the arrival, not the arrangement of these slips of paper—all of it came together at the conclusion of the day. It all sank down and was submerged into these questions, and we took these pictures away with us. I remember that when I showed it to Anton, I felt myself unusually set off from him. I had, after all, been there and he had not.[20] But the picture lay before the both of us. For me, the entire time of its unfolding was filled, while for him, it was

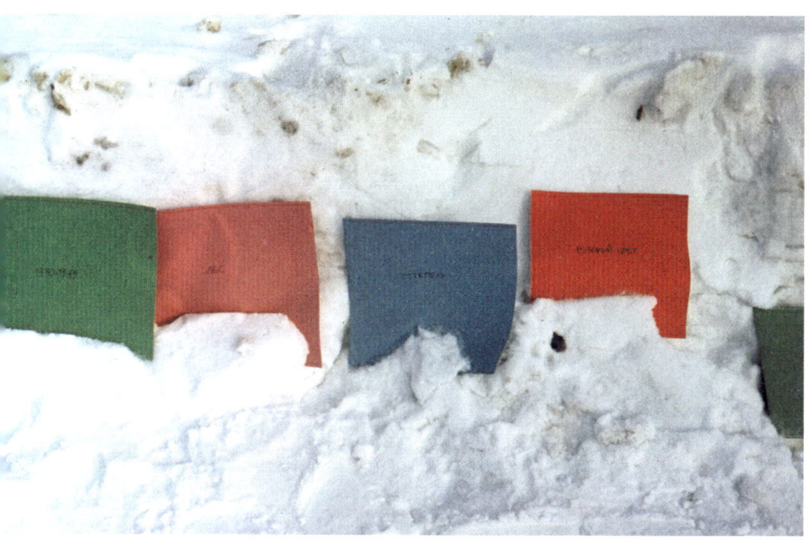

Fig. 32

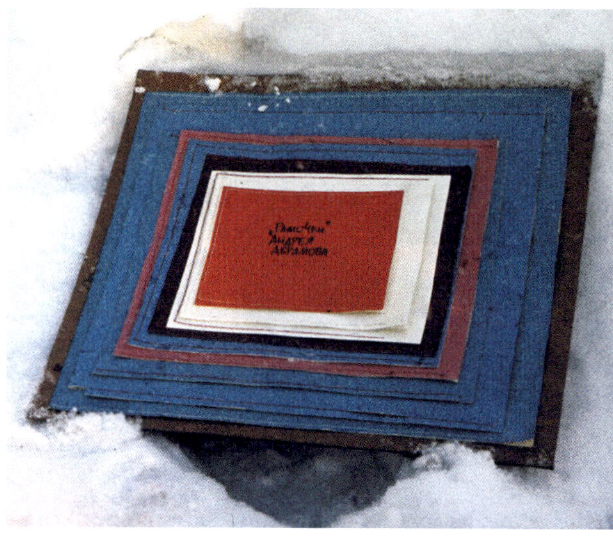

Fig. 33

a simple piece of paper like any other iconographic schema, reproduction, etc. This is when I understood the difference between myself and someone who has not seen. It is wonderful that this thing itself was the sign of that moment, i.e. the moment when I know but cannot say it to anyone, because it is impossible to convey. Another sees the same thing, but in fact does not know any of it. Curiously, though, the beauty exists for both me and him. This beautiful, rainbow-colored, four-sided armature is, for me, replete with content, while for him, it is filled simply with formal geometric beauty.

When we were all pasting these pictures together, the participants' departure had already taken place. They faded away into the spirit of Kio, the illusionist.[21] There was no thought of applause or desire to look for them, because my attention quickly and sharply switched onto myself, onto all of the procedures, onto my neighbors, and so forth. That is why when the participants left, I thought, so they left, and so what? They had not made any impression whatsoever, had not figured into it—everything had been switched to inner experience. The game itself, the journey, the snowy day,

20. Anton Nosik (b. 1966), Kabakov's stepson.
21. Igor Kio (1944-2006), famous illusionist from a family of Soviet magicians with the name Kio.

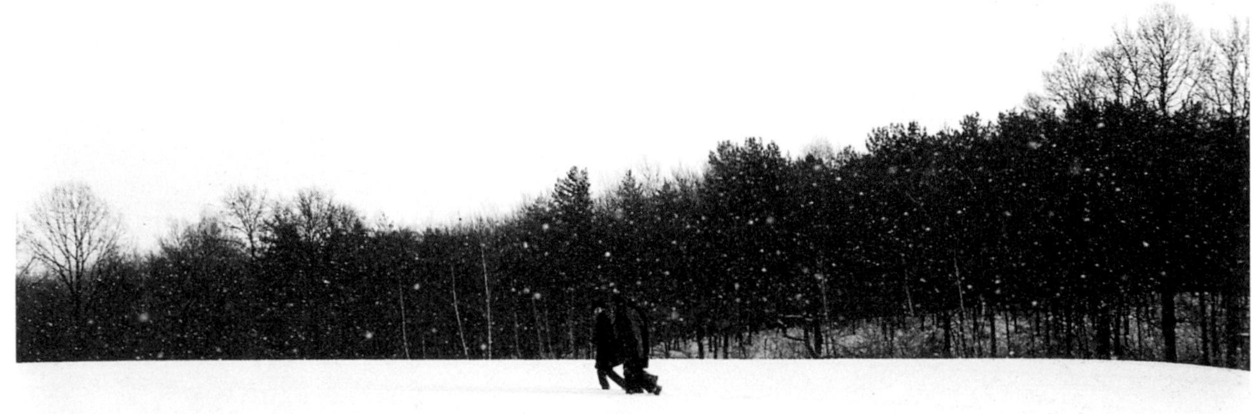

Fig. 34

everyone in their winter clothes; and what's more, everyone coming for the sake of this trifle, this nonsense. Over there, they go on some business, while we are here for the sake of nonsense—this again creates that sense of unity. It is remarkable that this many people come simply for the sake of nonsense, while others do not come for nonsense, but on a task. The moment of this isolation and rupture created an environment, a niche into which the entire event could fit. Anticipation was rewarded. The result that emerged was provided for and seemed to lie down in the crater, the cavity, which dovetailed with the filling of this cavity.

Then afterward, the effect of this gift produces a staggering impression, as though we had been present at the production of this gift, as though we had made our own day by spending the time, and the time linked up and turned into the gift of this task. Here, it seems, the general situation and the essence of the gift reveal themselves, because the gift is not a commercial transaction of the sort: you spend your time—now here, have a sandwich. Here, there is only memory—a souvenir of pleasantly spent time.

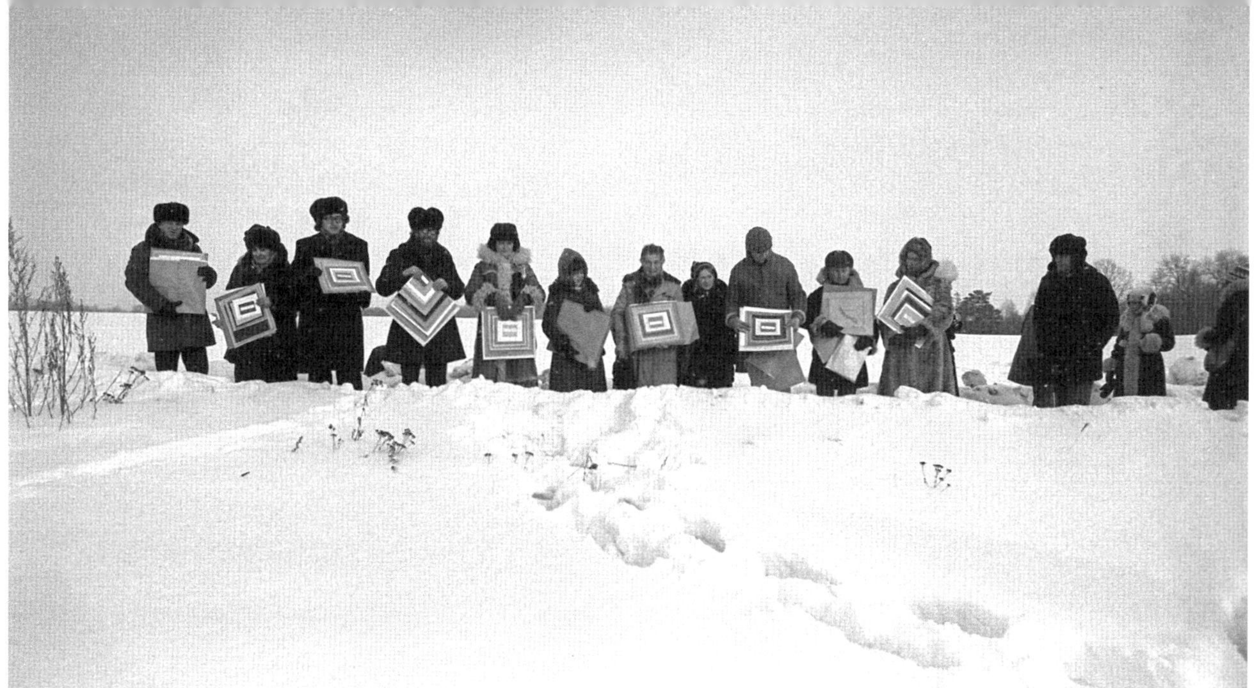

Fig. 35

I would define the general character of all these things as actions around pre-anticipation and the performance of a miracle. And moreover, not a disclosure followed by the return of the miracle into a deception—that it is just a piece of paper and nothing else, but precisely that a miracle is anticipated and then takes place. And each time, the miracle takes place in different spheres, but it takes place every time.

Oddly enough, this reminds me of going to the academy of music when a touring artist comes to visit. The difficulty of obtaining a ticket, having to arrive on time, and then the coat check—all of these agonizing situations. And could it possibly be that he would play a trick on me, with all the time and effort that I spent? Finally, a person comes out. You are watching him with a fiery gaze. Could it be that that person there, that fat or thin, or horrid, or ugly one, that he could do something right now that is the very thing for the sake of which I came? It does not look hopeful. This violin is oddly shiny, this familiar place is so tedious, and it is difficult to breathe, it is so stuffy. All told, nothing but anticipation itself and promise bodes of anything at all. Everything is perfectly prosaic. Well, of course, the lights are up and the harp has been polished, but this is still no guarantee. And then comes the most important moment: the conductor starts to wave his baton, that one there has raised his horn, another his violin, you seem to be waiting to see if he will be able to do anything with you. The fact that he will be doing something is clear, but will he be able to do this piece with me? Here there are grave doubts, though you seem to be completely ready for this to happen. This situation here is akin to these actions.

Setting aside the small mishap in *The Third Variant*, which we can omit, since the idea of the piece works on its own, this anticipation and the fulfillment of this anticipation in different spheres are what is completed. And sure enough, Stern[22] squeaks, and from his squeaking emerges something incomprehensible, but thanks to which you can go home satisfied.

From the very first time, I had the thought that everything that is taking place is taking place "inside of me." These things all maintain distance, silence, time, extension, the element of myth, unexpectedness—an entire series of demonstrational conditions is observed that creates the impression that what is taking place is taking place "inside" the viewer, and not outside. There is no need to look outward. On the other hand, the emotions that the viewer experiences are not forced—there is no pressure in the form of physical or mental torment.

22. Isaac Stern (1920–2001), Ukrainian-born American violinist who famously toured the Soviet Union in the 1950s.

Chuikov's Story: *Time of Action, Pictures, Place of Action*
Ivan Chuikov, July 1980

For me, these works are unified by a certain singular point of view. Evidently this is connected with my own personal interests, which is natural. Everyone considers these works within his own personal context. For me, this context is related to a certain miracle that takes place when perceiving a work—what I, for myself, call illusion. Illusion is what allows you at a certain point, when you realize that something is an illusion and connect it to what is taking place, to experience revelation. This experience of revelation is, it seems, the only thing that is truly interesting in any work.

I shall begin with "the rope" (*Time of Action*). This work is very pure and complete, without any secondary layers or secondary ideas, which is something I like very much. We came to the field and saw a rope lying across it. Then we began to pull it. Nothing else happens, it is all fairly dull and monotonous. The first thing that comes to mind when you begin to make sense of what is taking place, to interpret while still in the middle of the action, is time, the sweep of time, pure action. But these are all speculations, this is not what works. What works (and this happens unexpectedly) has to do with the imagination—you imagine this entire rope for yourself. But this image does not come all at once. At first, I thought that perhaps something would appear. Someone might come out, something might be pulled out; I had a few conjectures. But fairly quickly, it becomes clear that the point is precisely this, the action itself, it is action as such, pure action. But this is again rationalization, and apparently the kind that comes later, after direct experience. (I do not think I knew the title *Time of Action* at that point.) Whereas what you experience in the moment of action is very difficult to properly express in words, and the closest approximation of the revelation that I experienced there is simply to say that I imagined the rope lying there. The point is that in such a situation, when you imagine this rope to yourself, there is an objectivization that takes place. Time is directly and objectively presented by this rope. It has transformed into a kind of spatial magnitude, lying there, imaginable. But this again is rationalization. Whereas the point is precisely in the imagining, the image, and the illusion. Of course, a kind of illusion, a kind of miracle, even though there seems to be nothing miraculous in it. But sure enough, it is a miracle, because there is a revelation. For me, it happened instantly, close to the end of the action, and this became the meaning of the work, the thing that it gave me. And what is very interesting is that you understand immediately the impossibility. The whole rope cannot be on the ground, because you could not pull it all and it would break. In any case, all of this is clear, but that is precisely where the miracle lies. You imagine it receding, and since its length is unknown, you could imagine it to be infinite, you could be pulling it for a day, for two, for three. It recedes into the unknown. This is what worked.

•　•　•

I say—an illusion. It happens differently in *Pictures*. There, it is a simple substitution. The game is very interesting, what we were doing with the envelopes. As far as I remember, there were inscriptions and instructions related to the task at hand, which corresponded to the facts of the event—the weather, the place, I think, the time. There were descriptions related to the objects that we were holding in our hand, to the pictures themselves. There were also inconsistencies. The green one had the inscription "purple," and so on. And so, after the first two envelopes, you just start to play the game. Or to put it more precisely, you are being played with, but you are interested in what you will encounter and to what degree it will correspond, first with your expectations, and second with that reality to which they refer. And then, it was all just simply very beautiful. The beautiful pictures arranged in

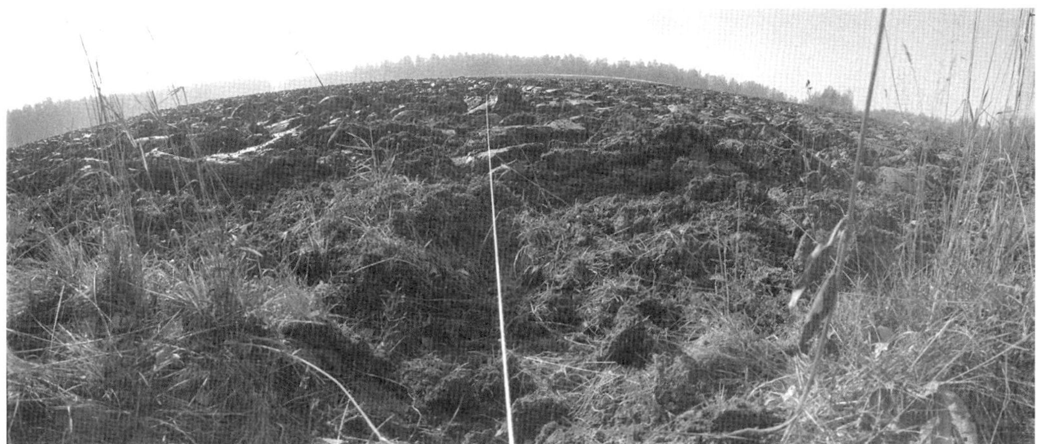

Fig. 36

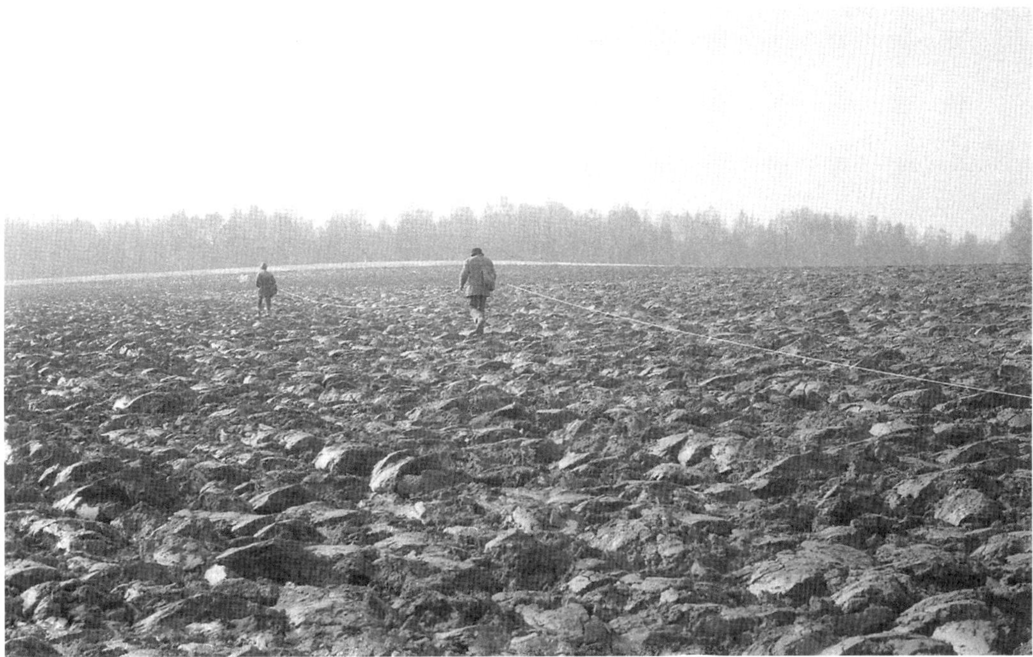

Fig. 37

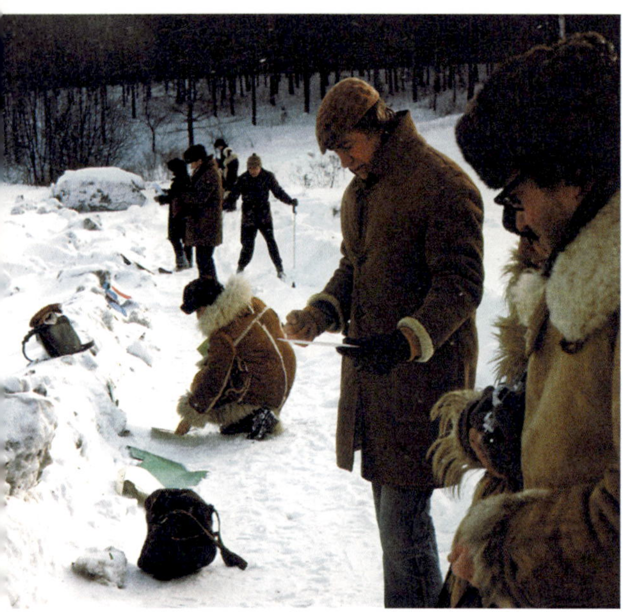

Fig. 38

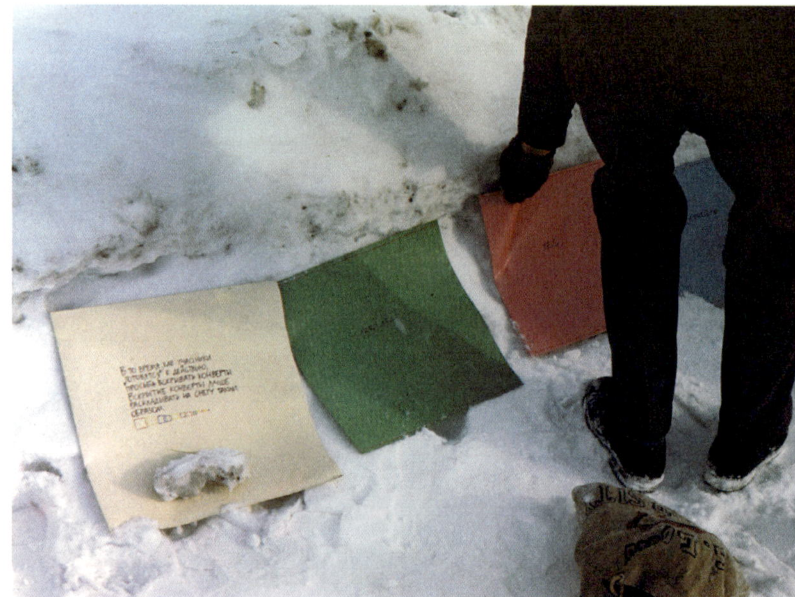

Fig. 39

23. Many of Chuikov's own paintings explore the illusion of pictorial perspective and the tension between illusion in painting and in real objects.

the snow, this was extraordinary. And then you suddenly discover that it was all a cover, a lie, that, in fact, the meaning does not reside in this at all, but somewhere else. (Actually, I happened to see the participants leaving, but did not pay any attention to it, thinking that they had simply stepped away somewhere.) This is the moment of epiphany, the flash, because you understand that you have been duped. You have been played with, but it was not hurtful, you are not irritated. It was fun, all the more so, since the situation was very pleasant, you could even say lyrical. And the people gathered there were friends. This unexpected turn took place in a very positive context. It was all very pleasant, but you understand that it was an illusion, some kind of fictive situation. You were presented with one thing, when in reality something else was taking place. All of this interested me, too, because it corresponds to the thing that occupies me all the time.[23] It is possible that there are other interpretations, but for me this was the most important one.

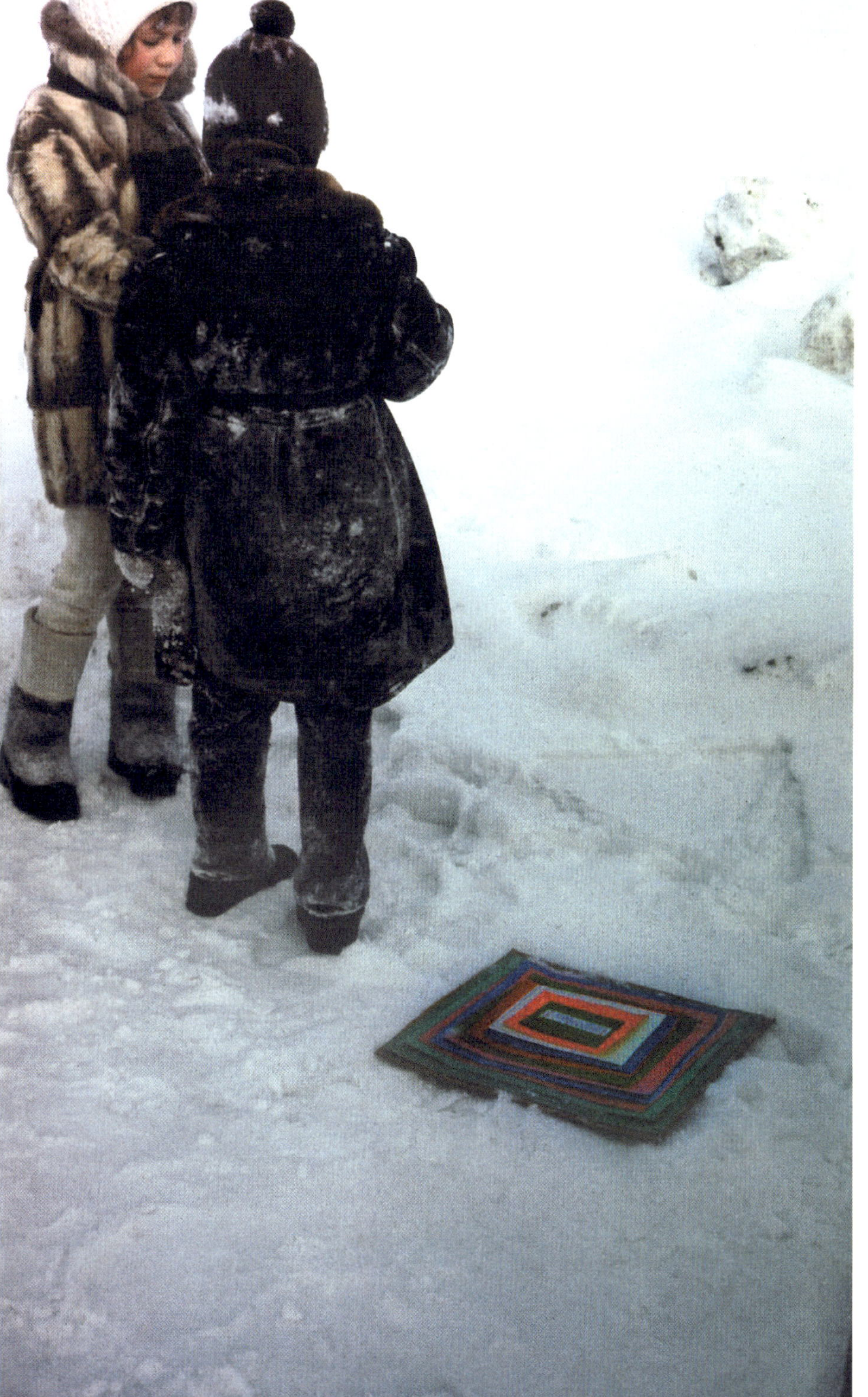

Fig. 40

And finally, even though I was did not go to *Place of Action*, I also want to say a few words about this work. For me, it is also connected to revelation, and this did not happen when I saw the documentation, nor when someone who had been there described the action to me. From the description, I understood that I did not understand anything: I understood the diagram, but did not see the point. There was no revelation until somebody said the phrase: "zone of indistinguishability." Andrei's presentation, which was fairly programmatic, was no explanation.[24] But just these three words. Then everything fell into place, everything clicked like a lock and there was this flash. (But here, since I was not present at the action, I do not know what I am missing.) In contrast to *Time of Action*, this work is extremely multi-layered. The main pivot, the moment of revelation, is wound up with many other layers. And it is very interesting (especially because I had not been there) to listen to the presentations of the different participants. They were themselves divided between those who had walked and those who had not walked. Thus, a comparison occurs: what

24. Chuikov is referring to the slide-film portion of the action, which included a tape-recording of Monastyrski's commentary and took place several weeks after the action in the field.

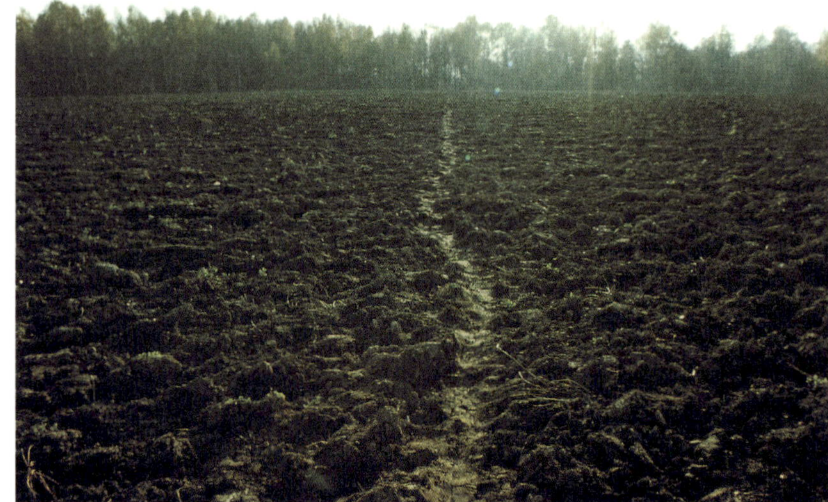

Fig. 41

those who had walked experienced, and how this was perceived by those who had not. The "zone of indistinguishability" more likely remained for those who watched. Those who walked acquired a completely closed, hermetic experience: they are able to share their impressions with each other, but cannot in any way share them with those who had watched but did not walk. Here again we find that same illusion as something conceptual: it appears as a second layer, as the comparison of incomparable things. After this the third layer is the slide-film, then the fourth is what took place in Igor's studio. And so it builds up like a snowball—you could continue to infinity. But I think that such an expanding work would have been more interesting if it had been constructed around an empty place. If inside, this snowball contained emptiness. But this, I think, is a combination of two works: the first is what makes up the center, the action itself, and the second is one that consists of many layers. I do not know whether this is a shortcoming, since multi-layered things have a chance at a longer life inside a person, at a longer period of analysis and interpretation. A monolithic thing remains undeveloped: it flashes and remains this way. There is a possibility of some kind of development.

I would like to underscore once more that every work contains a revelation, but it always takes place on the level of subjective viewer consciousness. In each case, the most important thing is the image that the viewer has, and this does not yield to description.

Kabakov's Story: *Place of Action*
Ilya Kabakov, November 1980

I will now try to remember that day, not to recount what actually happened, but rather, to give a sense of what the person who has been invited and the one who comes imagine.

We boarded the commuter train in the middle of the day, mostly all friends and acquaintances. We exited the train, crossed the railroad bridge, and saw that the bus that we would take was already waiting. We boarded it, and it stood for a long time without a driver. Some of us began to exit the bus into the street, but then the bus driver appeared and we all got back on again. There was a big crush, and the bus started going. The feeling that we were riding somewhere unknown and that you were completely released from all tasks was extraordinarily pleasant and peaceful because of the contrast with the usual state of being pre-programmed and preoccupied.

Finally, the bus stopped at a turn and the whole crowd of us got off the bus and started walking along the road. It was autumn. Although it was very damp, there was no slush or rain. It was very wet and very quiet—a true quiet autumn day. We walked along the road for some time (I remember that two cars went past), and then in quick succession turned off onto some muddy road and entered the forest. We walked through this forest single file, one behind the other. All around us were trees and the quiet, grey weather. It was nice not to think, and that some piece of time would be completely cut out and not included in your history.

We came out very quickly, did not walk long or wander. Before us was the field, and in the distance, far away, was another forest. This slightly

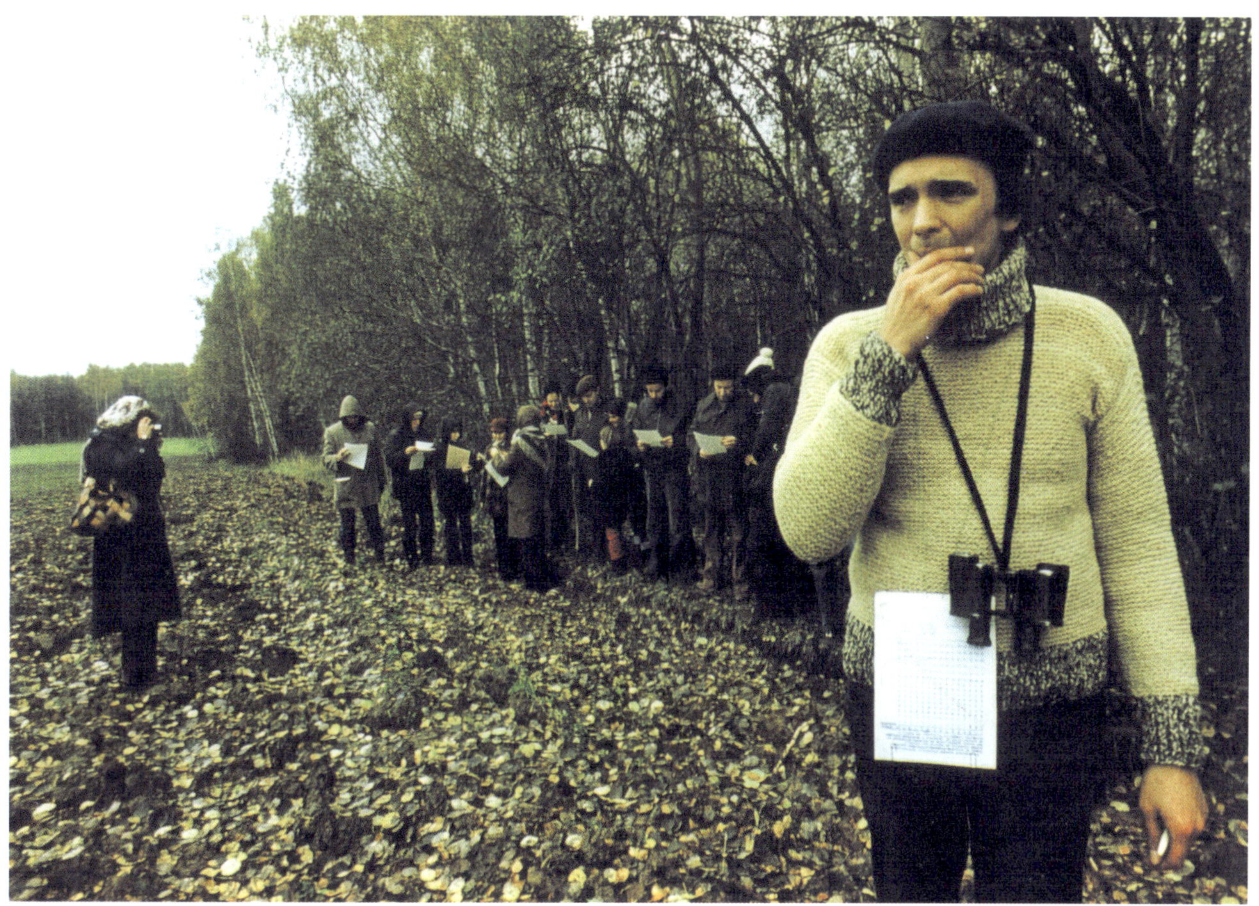

Fig. 42

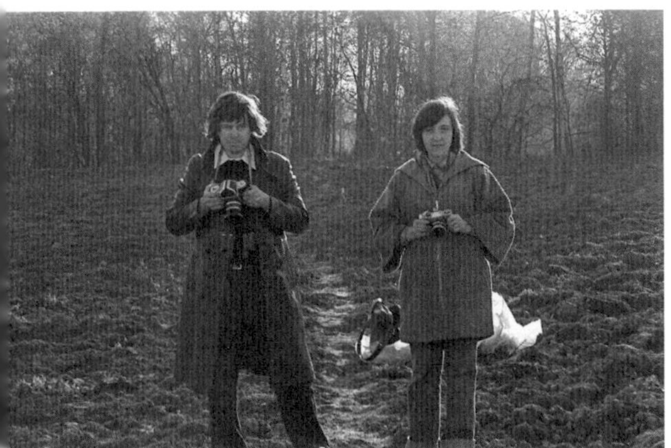

Fig. 43

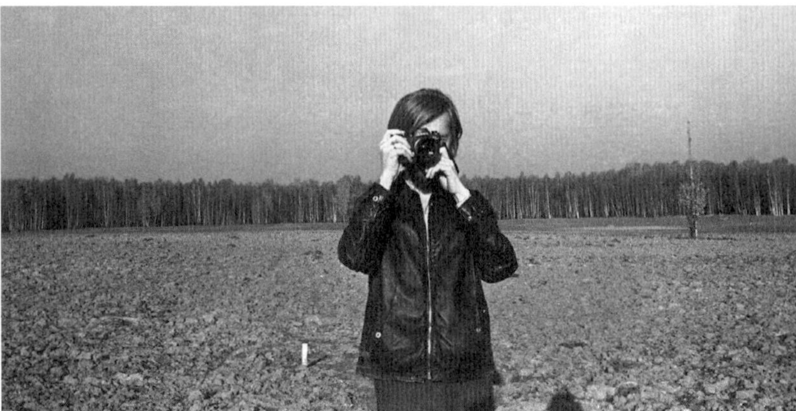

Fig. 44

hump-backed field with its tilled soil, perhaps already turned over again, was completely empty.

We lined up on one edge—I would say, like the French before the Battle of Borodino—wondering what lay ahead, but there was nothing special there. It was simply empty.

Andrei, in conference with Igor, was setting up the camera and constantly looking into the distance in the direction of the other forest. Evidently, some sort of program was being prepared. Well, let them arrange all this, we will just calmly stand here. Finally, Andrei, with a binocular around his neck and an umbrella in his hand, began to call the participants one by one. These participants were far away, they were receiving some instructions, something was happening, but since we were standing in a crowd to the side, we were sooner conversing amongst ourselves than participating. And then Andrei called me over, too. I walked up to the camera where Igor and Andrei with the binocular and umbrella stood, and was told that I should make my way across the field toward that forest over there, and I must do it in a particular way. It turned out that a kind of crude footpath had been trod in the slimy and fairly loose dirt field. It stretched away from the camera and into the distance. You could spot the first little stakes on the path. They retreated

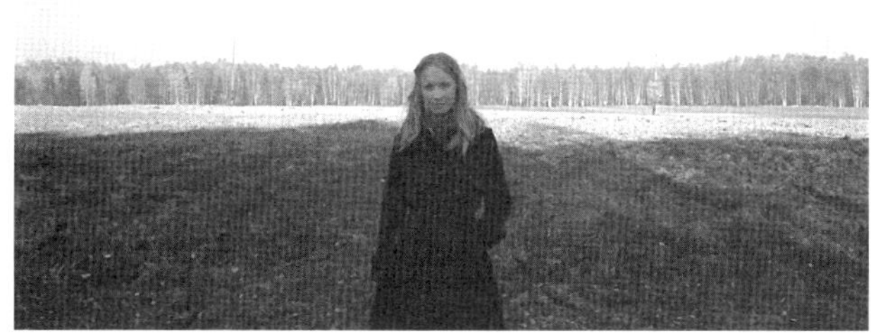

Fig. 45

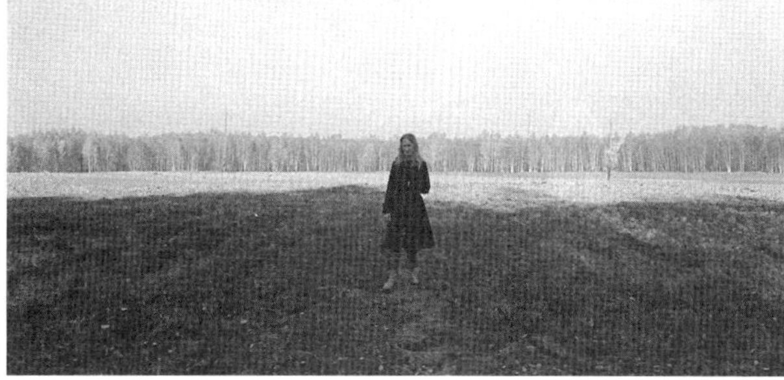

Fig. 46

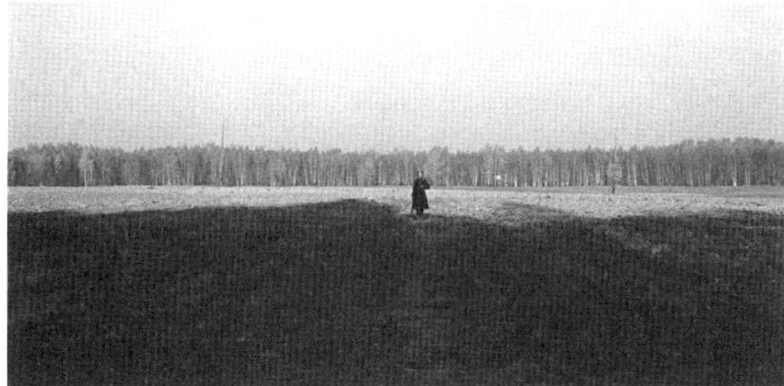

Fig. 47

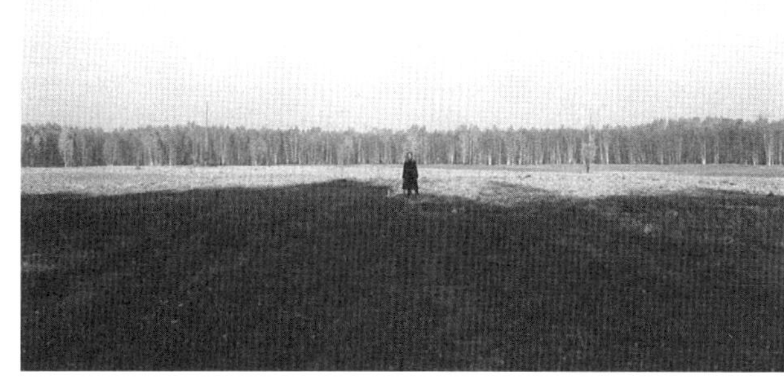

Fig. 48

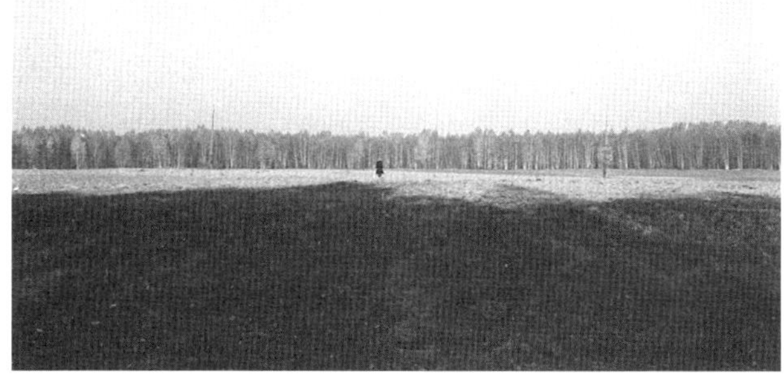

Fig. 49

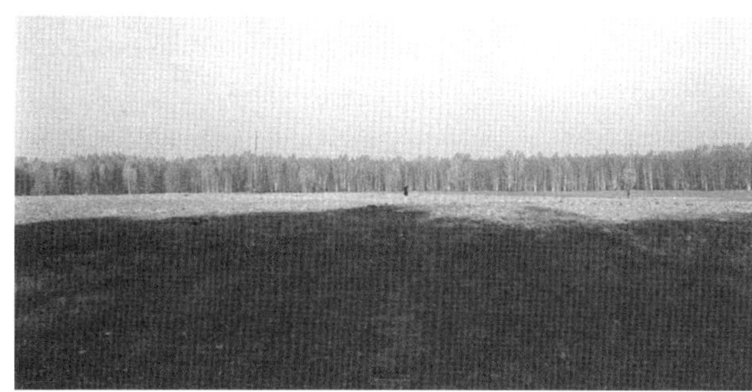

Fig. 50

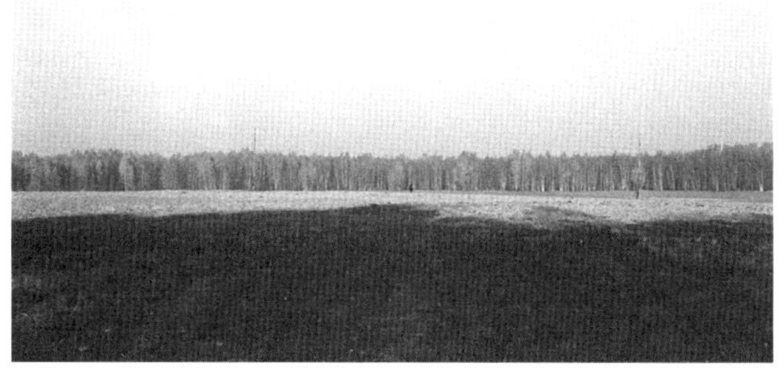

Fig. 51

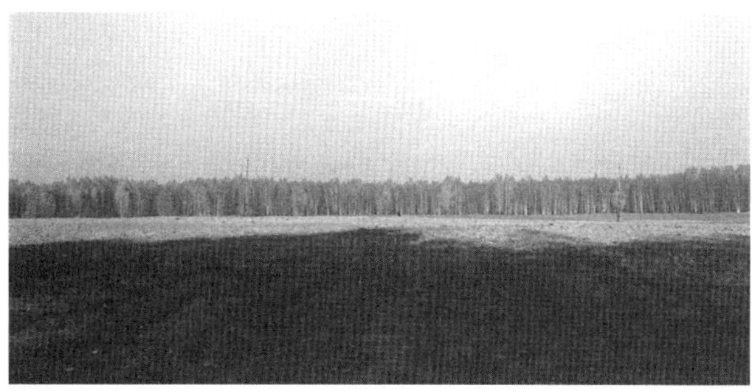

Fig. 52

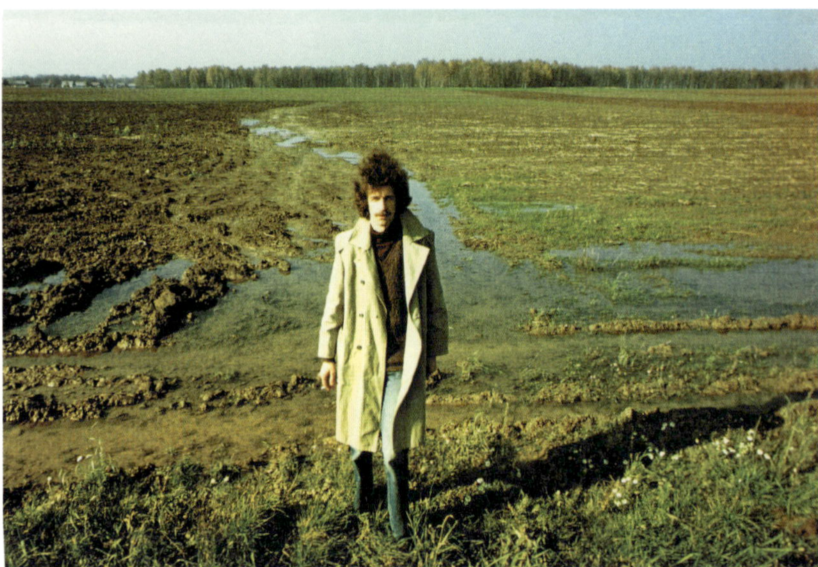

Fig. 53

away into the fog toward that far-off forest. Andrei instructed that, as I move through the field along the trodden, furrowed dirt path toward this forest, that I should stop alongside each little white stake and turn around in order to be photographed. And so I understood that I must stop next to each stake and turn around, but in essence to move toward the forest. I asked what it was that was hovering impossibly far away, but Andrei said ambiguously that in any case, it would become clear later.

Well, this is what I did. I made my way across this field. I turned around by the first stake, then turned around by the second stake, all the while moving along the trod-down path toward the other forest. It should be said that each time I turned around, there was a strange effect of loss, of abandoning these close friends with whom I had just been standing. And now they were already very little. They stood by the forest and did not look at me at all. They did not look at me the same way that I had not looked, standing with them, at those others receding into the field. There was nothing special in

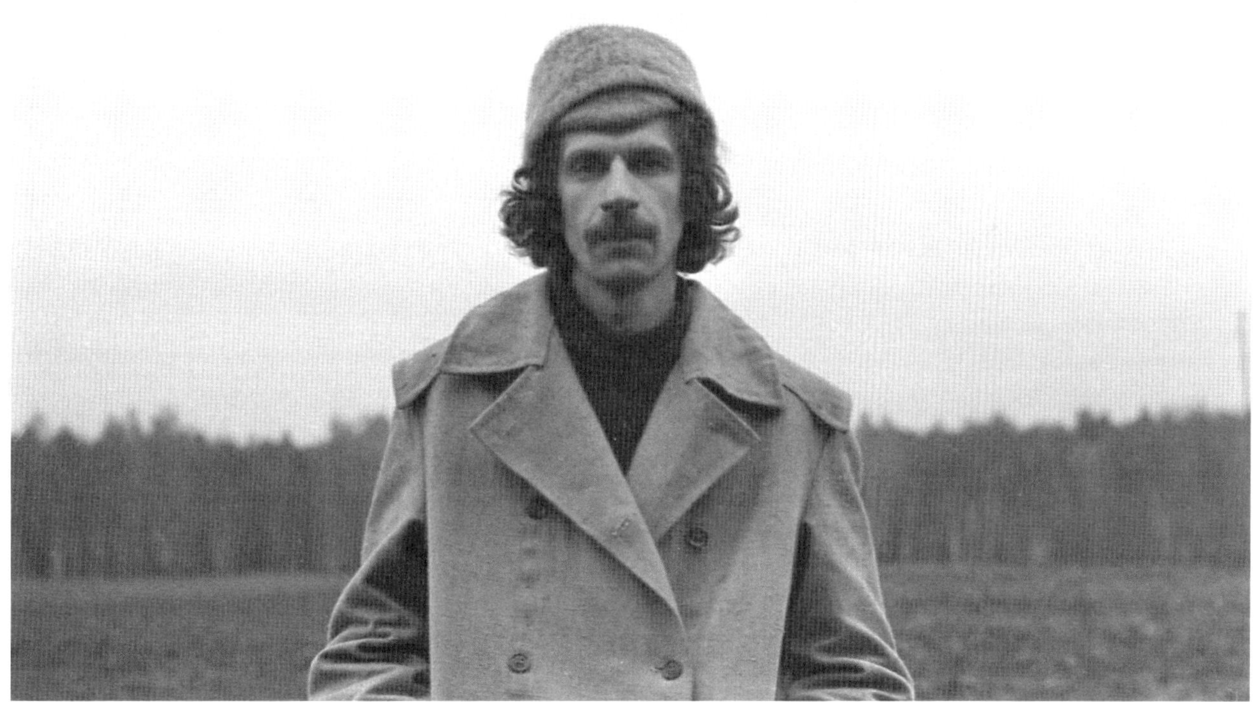

Fig. 54

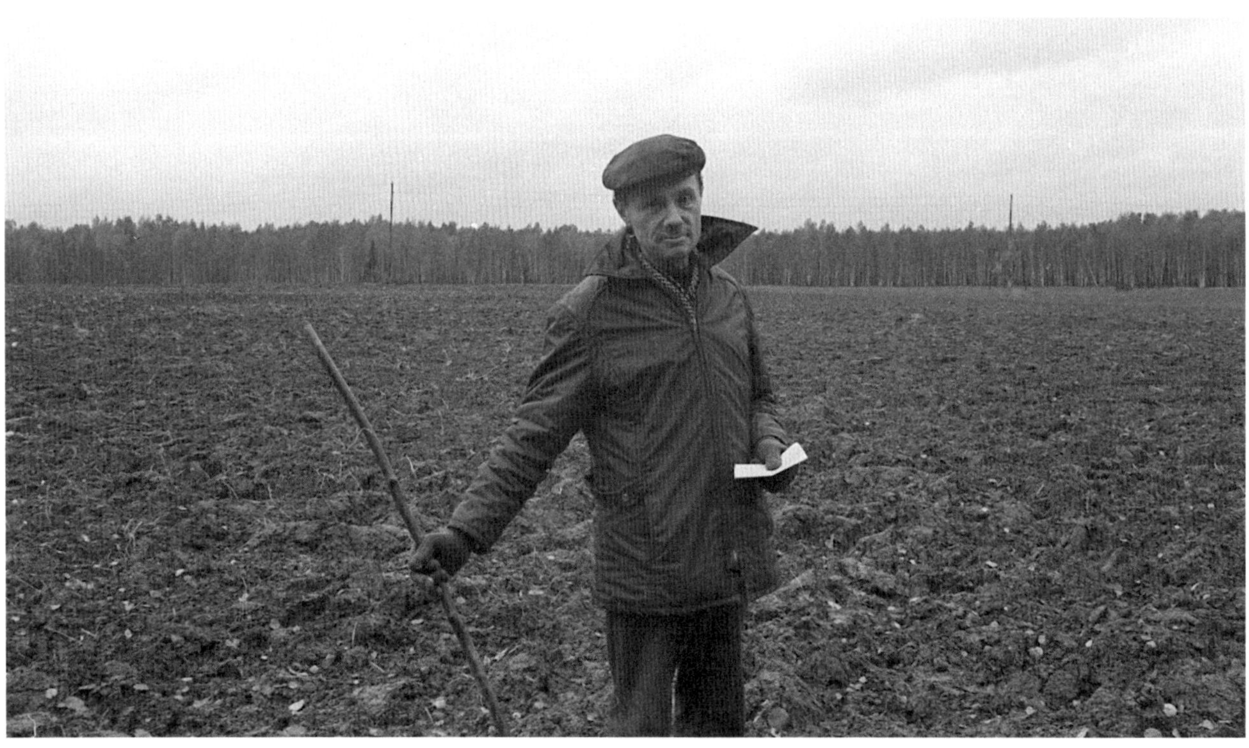

Fig. 55

this, but it seemed to produce an impression nonetheless, the fact that they paid no attention whatsoever to me as I moved down the field. Finally, they transformed completely into tiny grouplets, then became indistinguishable: Andrei and Igor, and the friends—and that was all. And I found myself alone, moving along this field. I should say that it was fairly large to try to cross quickly. Therefore, I spent an enormous length of time in the middle of this dirty tillage between the two edges, as if in some kind of extraordinary emptiness. But at the same time, I was moving at someone's request and along a predetermined course. And so, I knew clearly that I would not veer off course, but would make my way along this trodden little groove there, into the distance. And this state—of movement toward the unknown, but at the same time along a marked path with an incredible emptiness all around—created a very strong impression: a seeming trifle, but at the same time affecting. I acted of my own free will, with the unknown ahead of me, but this was not frightening—anyway, it is difficult to explain. This lasted

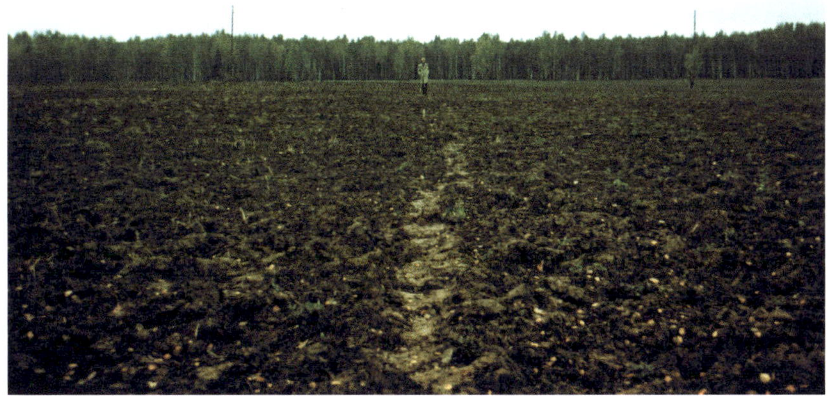

Fig. 56

a fairly long time, sufficient time was lost. I remember that I did not care very much where I was going, though the edge of the other forest gradually became clearer, and more importantly, even before this forest edge, there was something purple that seemed to hang between two poles. But I did not get curious: who knows what could be hanging there? And just the same, turning beside each stake that appeared in my path, I slowly approached that purple thing. It turned out to be a purple curtain.

I must say that the impression from this curtain and the now-close forest edge turned out to be completely different from the impression we received when we arrived at the forest edge after the commuter train and bus. That was an event that was completely natural and part of life, while the event here—after crossing the field and approaching these new, completely real things, i.e. the curtain and the edge of the forest—felt like it came after some extraordinary experience. In fact, we could speak about a state close to sleep, since sleep diverges sharply from what we have in reality. And though this was the very same earth as before, after my passage through this emptiness, the appearance of these new things for some reason created the impression of existing in another psychic world. And so, I approached this curtain. I don't know what to say about it. I did not completely understand why there was a curtain here. The ambiguity of the curtain in the field felt completely natural, and I don't say this because it was some kind of contrived thing, but simply—well, so what, so it turns out that there's a curtain here . . . In other words, it was like in a dream when a cow is as big as a house—well, so what? In short, this curtain did not call up any of the expected feelings. Nevertheless, when I approached it—it is difficult to say whether calmly or with surprise, or maybe as in a dream with some kind of mild surprise—I saw that directly behind this curtain, in a ditch, lay Seva Nekrasov. But I repeat again that since I seemed to find myself in a new state, even Seva lying in a ditch in the earth did not surprise me in the least. Seva was inspecting something down there in the ditch. With a stick in his hand, he was aiming at me as if with some kind of machine gun. This is the impression I got. But none of this created any oppression or heaviness, first because Seva was smiling, and second, because, of course, I knew it was a stick—where would Seva get a machine gun like that? And anyway, this could not happen here, because everything was supposed to be strange, but pleasant.

As soon as I appeared at this ditch, Seva began to rise, first on all fours, and then, climbing to the edge and with a smooth gesture, he invited me to lie down in his place in the ditch.

But I have not said anything about this ditch. Do not think that it was a ditch full of dirt—nothing of the sort. It was an unusually comfortable ditch, this was immediately obvious. Its floor was covered with a plastic sheet to keep out the damp, while in the ditch itself laid a marvelous mattress. It was the kind that we all love to lie on at the beach or somewhere in the bosom of nature, as if to add a mass of pleasure and enjoyment to lying around in this nature that by itself either pricks or pinches, or something else that you are always expecting from it. Here the situation of comfort was provided for as much as it could have been in such conditions. But at the same time, the optical effect of the ditch was fully preserved.

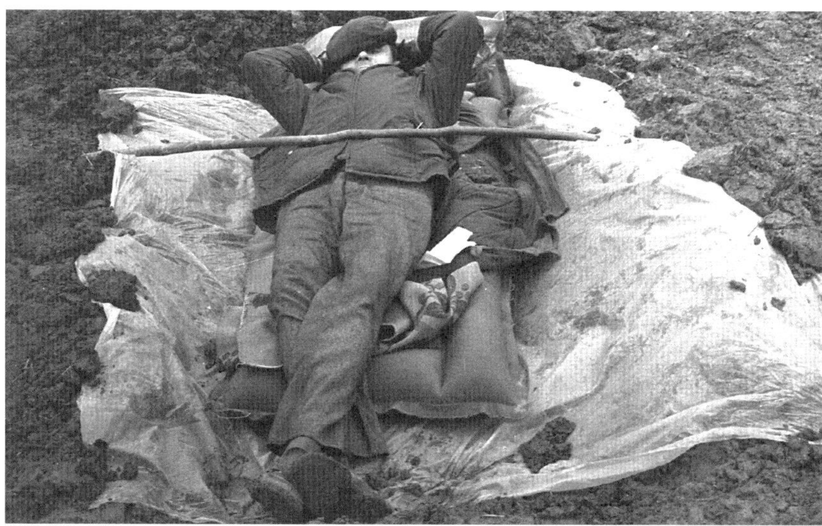

Fig. 57

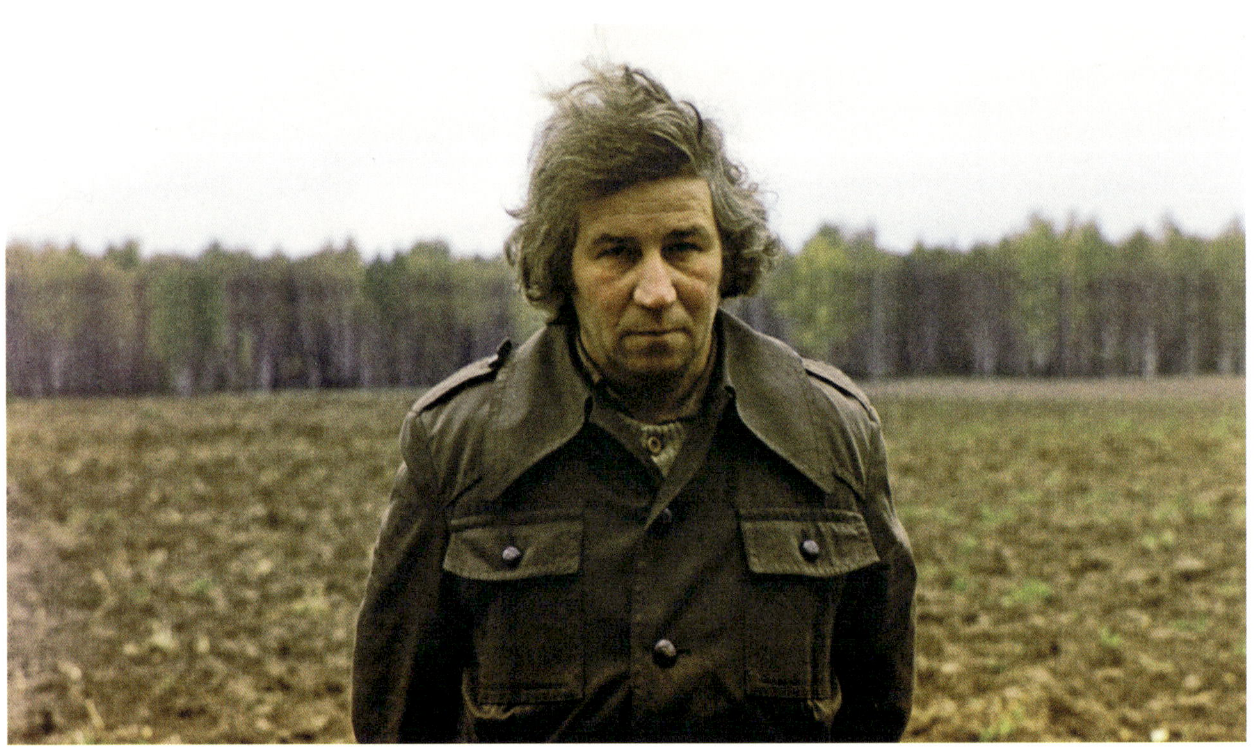

Fig. 58

Seva, wielding the camera, evidently wanted to capture my time in the ditch. Fumbling with the camera, he took a picture of me. (It turned out later that he should not have fumbled with it, as he just ruined it.) I instantly understood that I, too, should take a picture of whoever turned up in the ditch after me. After all of this, Seva withdrew in the direction of the other forest. I should note that the ditch was about fifty meters from the other forest's edge. And that is where the whole trick lies: the person thinks that he is at the forest's edge, but instead ends up in this ditch, right there behind the curtain.

And so I lay down in the ditch. I cannot say that I gazed at the sky while lying in this ditch. I simply rested there quietly; you could say that I was just lying around. I understood that somebody must be coming now of those friends remaining on the other shore, but for some reason I had no desire to know who it might be. I simply lay and waited for the moment when someone would come So that in essence, I was busy lying in the ditch and had no curiosity about what would happen next or where Seva had gone.

When, by my supposition, enough time had passed and some character, some persona was supposed to appear, I peeked out of the ditch, turned, with even some dissatisfaction, and saw that approaching me was a lady in a fall cloak who, of course, did not know that I was lying in the ditch. But I had no desire to stare at what this lady would experience once she discovered the large ditch and myself in it—since, I repeat, the state of calm repose was the main thing.

And sure enough, the lady appeared above the edge of the ditch, but she did not show any particular surprise or shock upon seeing me. Hovering by the curtain, she began to inquire whether she should pull the curtain. I said, pull the curtain if you wish. I did not know her name. She began to pull it across. I said: it looks like it needs to be untied (the curtain was tied into a knot), you can probably leave it untied. It can just hang that way. But no, she carefully performed everything that was written (the curtain had a label saying that it should be untied and then later re-tied, which I had not done).

She did it all meticulously, for her own reasons, naturally. Then I told her to lie in the ditch, but she had figured it out herself anyway, that there was nothing left to do. She lay in the ditch and stretched out her booted legs. I did not fumble with the camera—I do not understand anything about cameras—and simply pressed the trigger to depress the shutter. And then, I remember, I placed it down carefully, didn't throw it—it's an expensive thing after all. After which I calmly, with the sense of a duty discharged, headed in the direction that Seva had gone.

The edge of the forest was already near. The slush on this side of the field, which, I repeat, was humped, had increased sharply; the well-trod and trampled path was almost all puddles. I jumped from mound to mound, but did not fall, though truthfully, my shoe was completely submerged in mud several times. Finally, I began to emerge onto the grass and to approach the edge of what was now a new forest. And here I saw a large group of people, naturally all familiar. I saw Erik, who was standing there, and I saw Seva.[25] I have to say that, from the first moment, I immediately had the feeling that all of this was taking place in another world. And I should say that he, too, asked me, laughing, how I liked it here in the other world. I said that it was very pleasant in this other world: first, it was all close friends and loved ones; second, I saw at once that there was a fire and that, if I was cold, I could warm myself. I was suffering from a terrible hunger and I asked if there was anything to eat. It turned out that there was something to eat: inside a transparent sack there were slices of bread and even some meat. I was experiencing an extraordinary happiness: first, I was in this other world, and second, it was so pleasant, so wonderful. But then I found that all was not so simple. I first had to go to this board. I don't remember who invited me, but in any case, there was a board right there nailed to a birch tree. I walked up to it. One of these "new-worlders"—that is how I would put it—was already standing by the board and reading carefully. I too started reading, but felt an extreme inability to read after the first line. Point A photographs Point B was the only thing I understood. Person E moves toward Point F. I must say that I even felt a pang at such a profanation of

25. Erik Bulatov (b. 1933), painter and close friend of Kabakov.

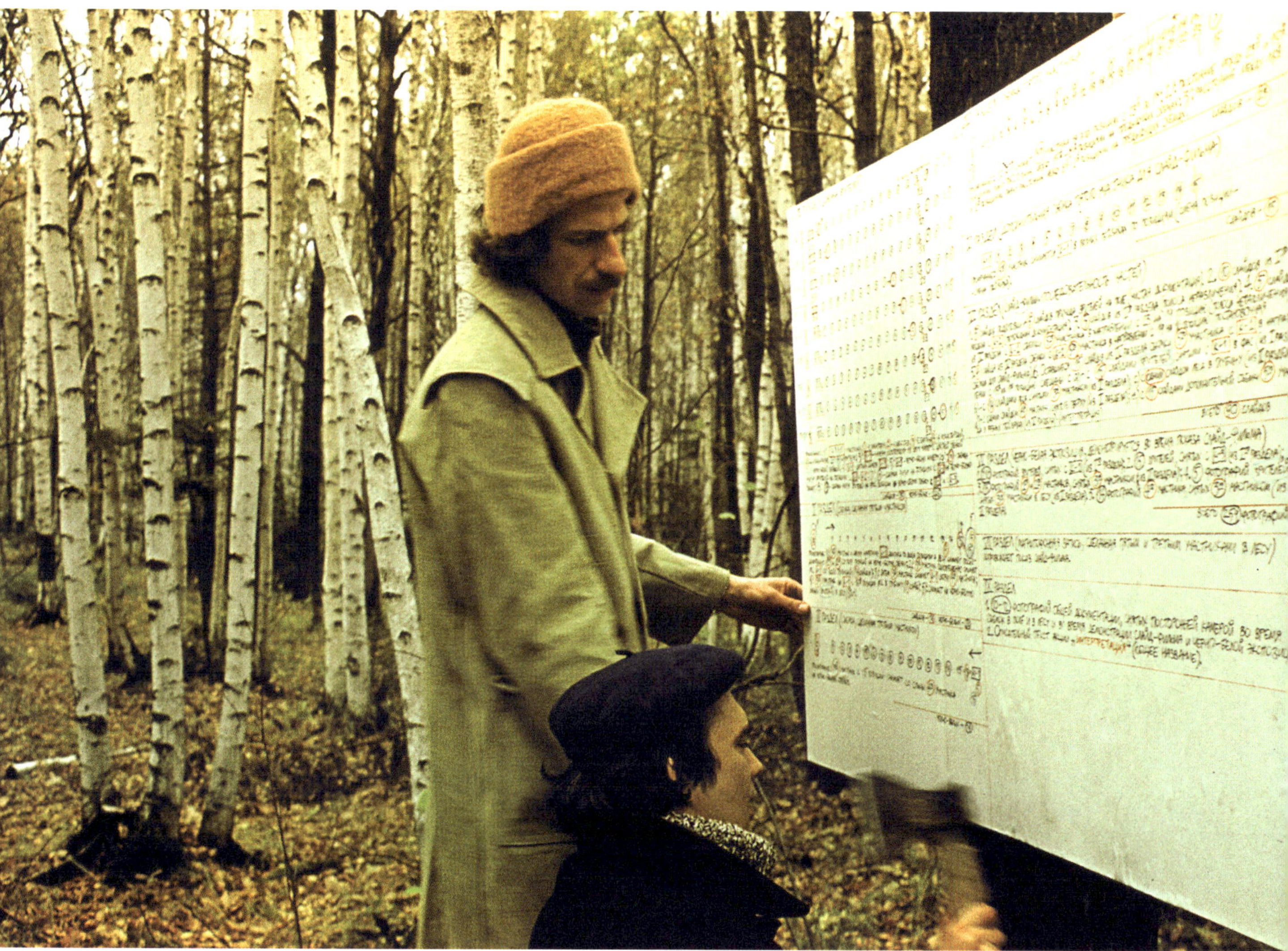

Fig. 59

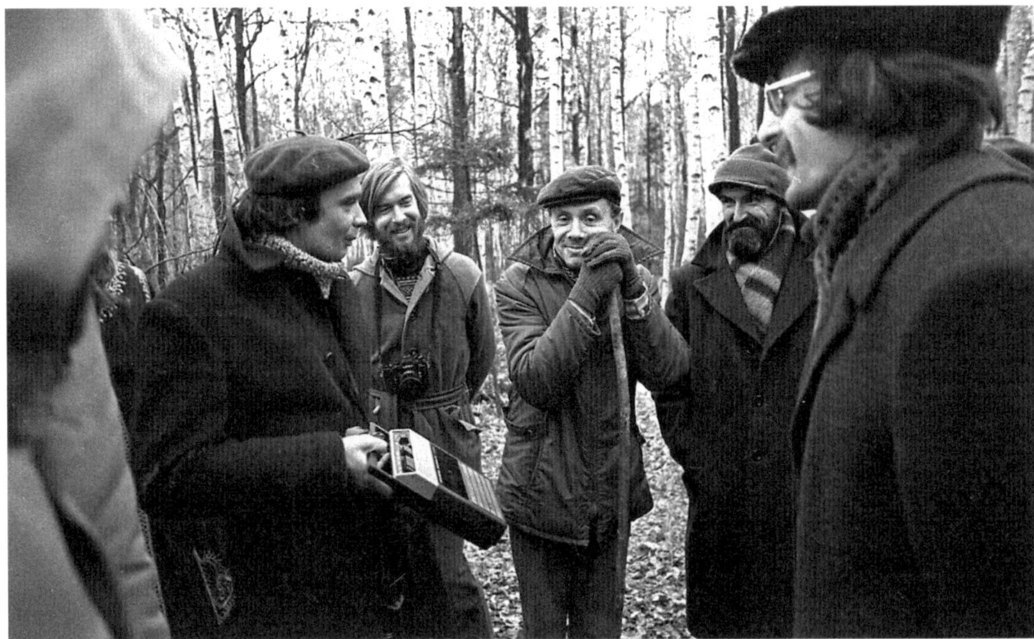

Fig. 60

the "other world." I am here practically post-mortem, I am practically flying, while here we are again accounting, re-accounting, the strict regimentation of everything that was taking place. Although, who knows, it must mean that such things exist here too.

I was full of pleasant sensations. I repeat, the experience of a mystery occurred, took place.

The lady who had lain in the ditch was already approaching, and someone else was lying in her place. In general, this sequence of events, this sequence of intervals was extremely pleasant. It was like suddenly seeing it in a dream, a constant, unavoidable stream, through this ditch over here, towards us, onto this forest's edge.

Here Erik suggested that, while everyone was crossing over from that side to this one, we take a stroll in the autumn forest. And so we went, the

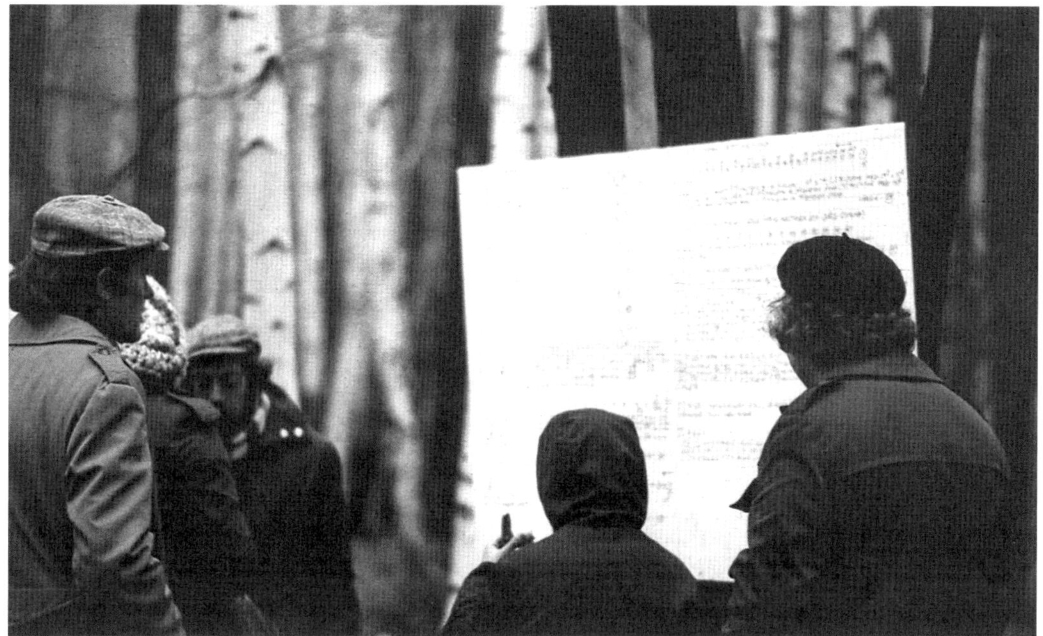

Fig. 61

three of us with Seva, talking quietly, mostly just rustling the leaves. Seva came upon two mushrooms and pinned them with a stick he had picked up. But there were no more mushrooms after that.

Then everyone crossed onto this forest's edge, started to mill around, to talk. Well anyway, everyone ended up here, on the other side. In essence, that's where all the experiences end—that's all there was that day. And after, we rode home on the commuter train.

Mironenko's Story: *Place of Action*
Vladimir Mironenko, June 1980

When we all got to the field, I did not experience any particular, individual sensations. Nothing was happening yet, just a group of friends and strangers getting ready to undertake something that was unknown to me.

I was the second in the order. That is, it turned out that there was one person ahead of me, and if for him it was a total mystery—because he was also not told ahead of time what he would have to do—then I, in the role of some kind of follower, did not experience this kind of uncertainty. I knew already that another person had reached that point and nothing sensational or frightening had happened.

When I began to walk along this field, for the first 50 steps I still sensed the people standing behind me. I felt their attention on me and was somehow tied to them. As I walked farther and farther away—this happened in stages and spurts, because I would stop, be given the signal, and continue walking farther—it was as though I was gradually being freed from these people's influence. The sense of a certain tension vanished and there appeared a sense that it was just me and there was no one else around. There was a sensation of vast space all around. The field was large and the weather was overcast, and it corresponded to this kind of mood. Probably the freest sensation I experienced was somewhere in the middle, between the point from which I started walking and where I was supposed to arrive, prior to the curtain.

Then, once again, I started to sense the nearing of something living and material. I saw the curtain. I suspected that there was someone there, and

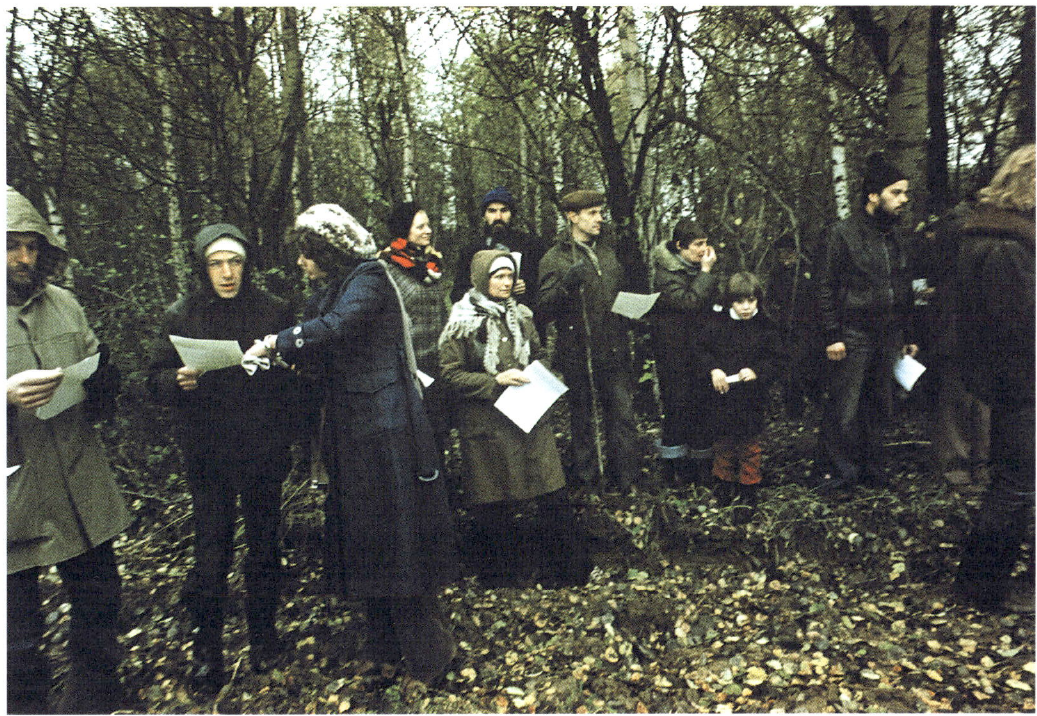

Fig. 62

that further on, in the forest, there were also people. It was as though I were already re-entering the world of people, but all of this was hazy. Still, I did experience a surprise when I opened the curtain and saw a person lying there. This was a strange pose, a strange angle, it even seemed kind of funny. Then I did what I was supposed to, since it was interesting and curious, and so I lay down in this ditch.

In the ditch I again felt myself—and to an even greater degree—severed from everything. I knew with absolute certainty that for the 10 minutes I would lie there, no one would bother me and I could do whatever I wanted—not in the sense of going away somewhere, but simply in that a sense of complete freedom appeared. This is what I decided: I knew that it had taken me about 10 minutes to cross the field, so the next person would come no sooner than in 10 minutes—thus I had 10 minutes at my disposal in which to contemplate what was taking place. And this is precisely what was pleasant to me.

I had been given the book *Russia in the Shadows*.[26] But for some reason it did not read easily, even though it was new to me. I tried to read, but it was completely impossible. It was significantly more interesting not to read this book, but just to be in a state of some kind of high, to experience the strangeness of the situation in which I found myself, the strangeness of the position in which I lay in this ditch—all of it was slightly absurd.

When the next person arrived and started to photograph me, I felt some kind of conspiratorial tone in our interactions, because we seemed to be engaged in the same task—not in the sense that we were engaged in some kind of deception, but in the sense that we were both performing a common task, while the others, who were on either side of the field, had nothing whatsoever to do with us.

When I stood up outside of the ditch and went to the "final" point of the journey, I began to join the common circle once again. But the sensation was completely different in comparison with what I had experienced standing on the field at first. When I stood at the beginning, at the first step, there was anticipation, the unknown. I did not know what would happen—the field is large, who knows what could be there, there could be ditches I could fall in—in short, all kinds of foolish thoughts arose. I did not know how everything would turn out—whether it would succeed or not.

And now there was the sense that something had already passed. And all these people were already different from those who had stood at the starting point on the other end of the field. They had experienced the same sensations that I had experienced, had walked the same path and were burdened by a knowledge, which the others, who still remained on the opposite side of the field, did not possess. Here, too, a kind of solidarity appeared; everyone smiled ironically and remained silent.

Now I will say a bit about this purple curtain. It naturally blocked me from those people at the end of the field who knew nothing, and it also

26. A series of articles by H. G. Wells written for *The Sunday Express* about his 1920 trip to Russia. The book was first published in the Soviet Union in the early 1920s and not reprinted until 1958.

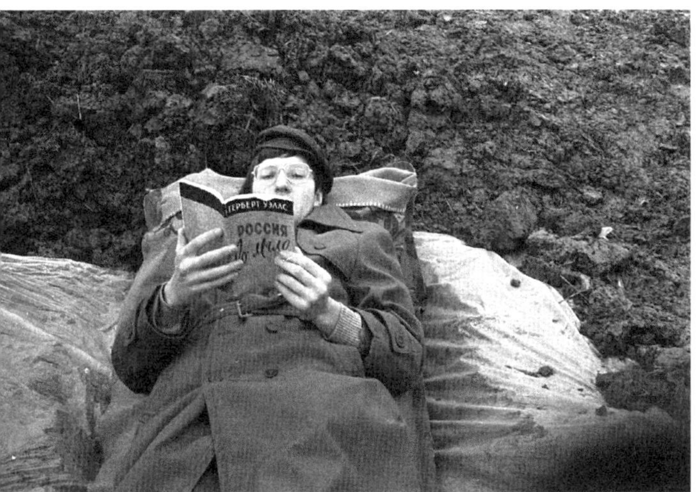

Fig. 63

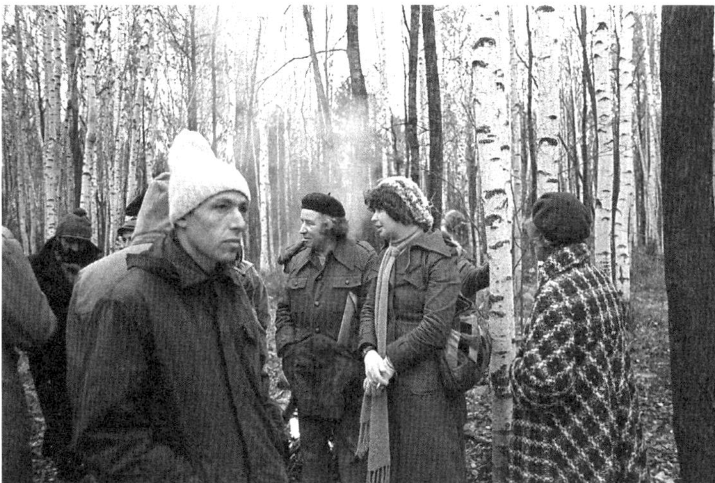

Fig. 64

served as a kind of cover or shroud that guarded me from those people at the starting point who existed in a kind of worldly atmosphere, who laughed, etc.; in other words, from the ordinary, unremarkable situation. During the time of my laying in this ditch, some kind of falling-out of memory took place. While I lay in the ditch, all of it seemed to be forgotten. I could not at the time formulate any concrete impressions; those came later. But in that moment, everything was good and I did not desire anything—it is a rare thing for me when I do not want absolutely anything, anything at all—all around was emptiness, silence, and an enormous sky. When you look up at it directly from below, it surrounds you on all sides. You rarely find yourself in such a pose in life.

In this way, a process of gradual forgetting began to take place. When I began to walk, I started to forget that there were people behind me, that conversations were and are taking place there. All of this disappeared somewhere as I walked farther and farther away. Then, again, with the approach of the curtain, a tension began to arise: there is something behind it, it could not just be there like that. In the first part, I was in movement, I was walking

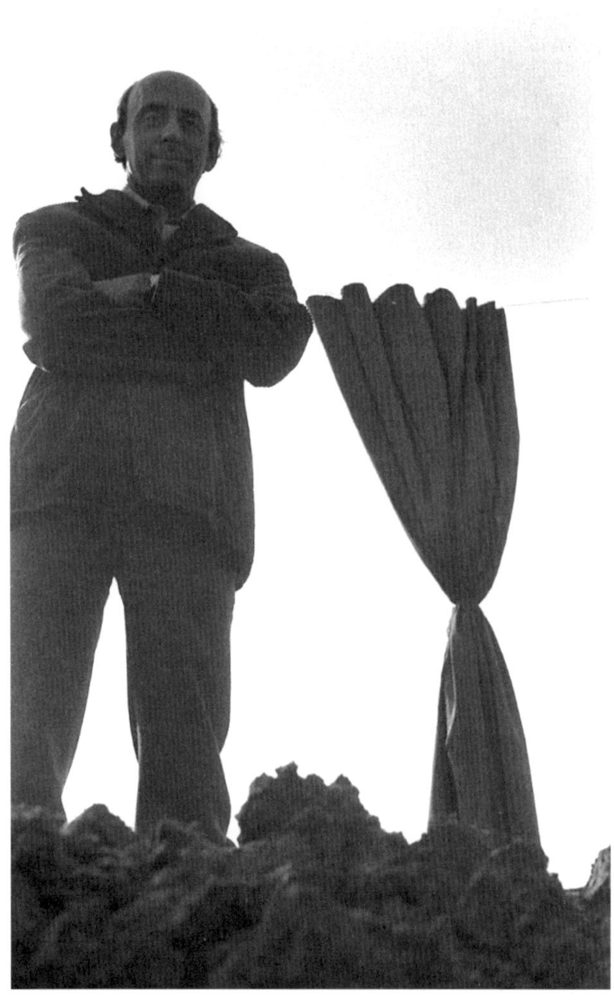

Fig. 65

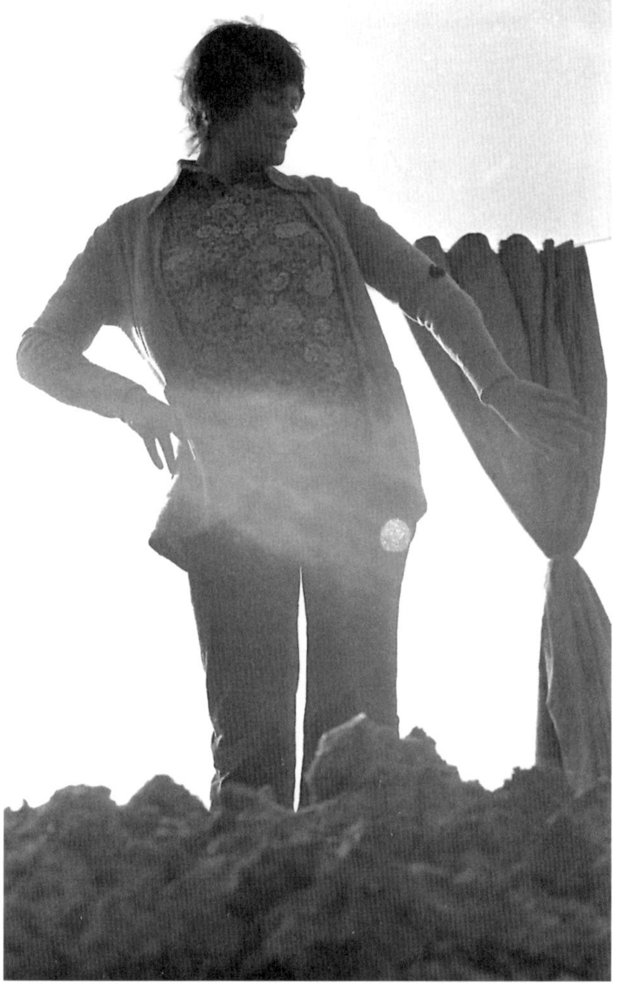

Fig. 66

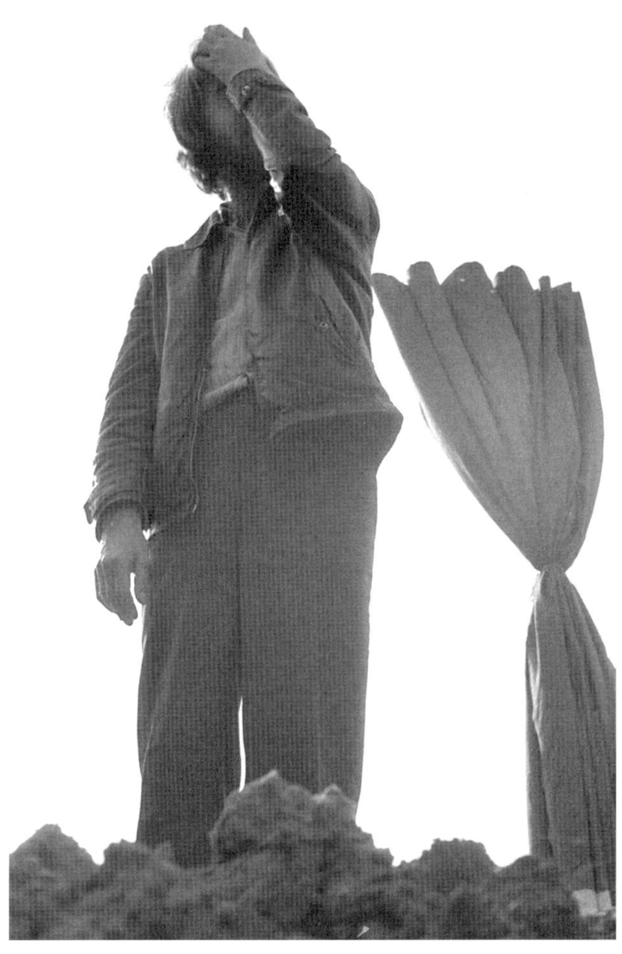

Fig. 67

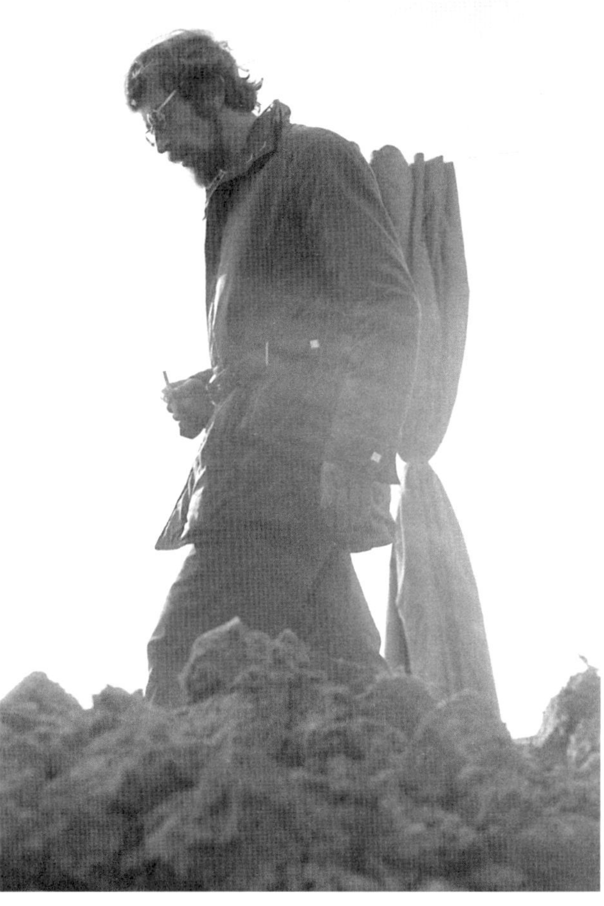

Fig. 68

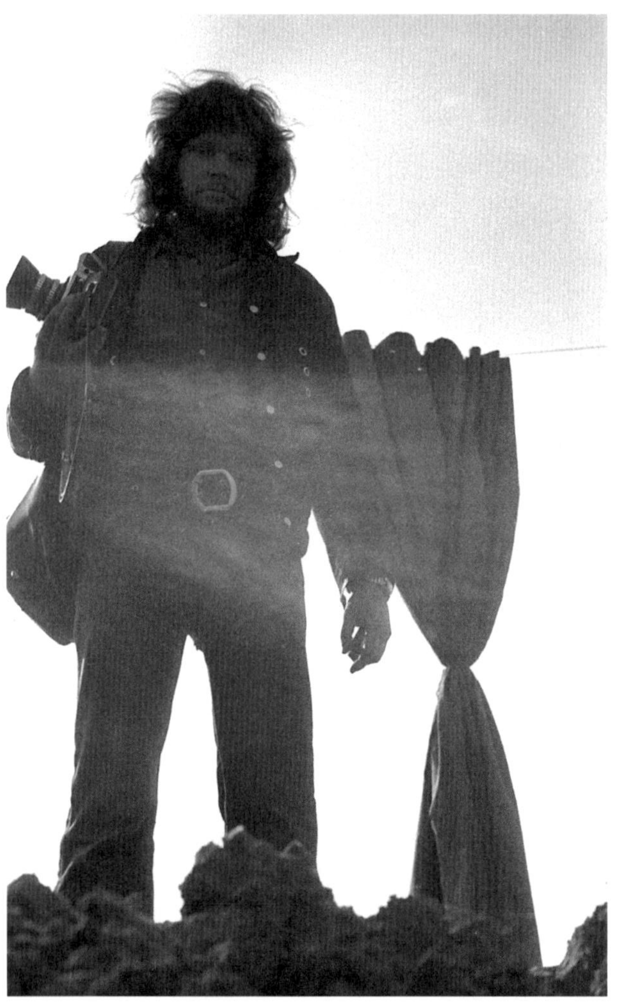

Fig. 69

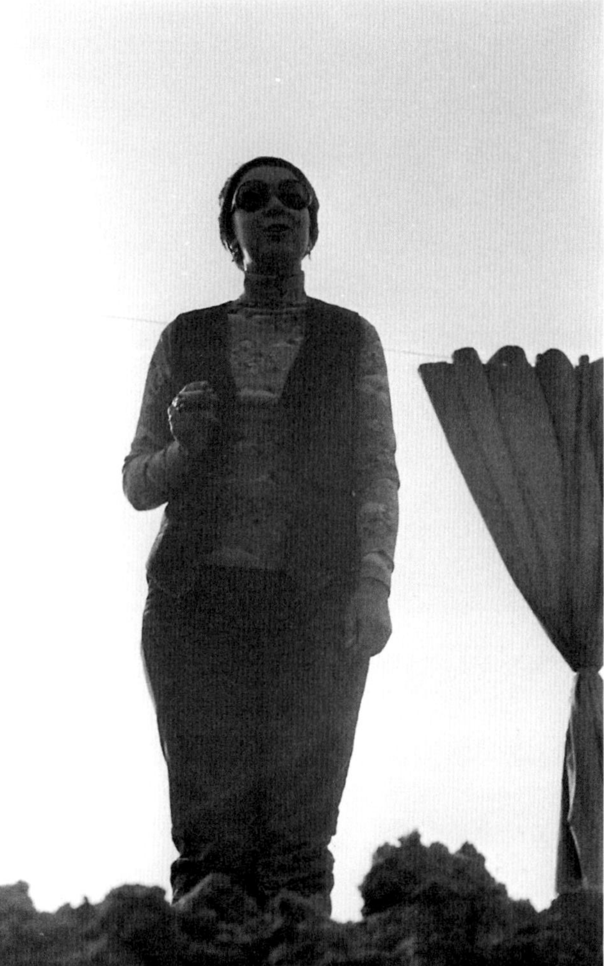

Fig. 70

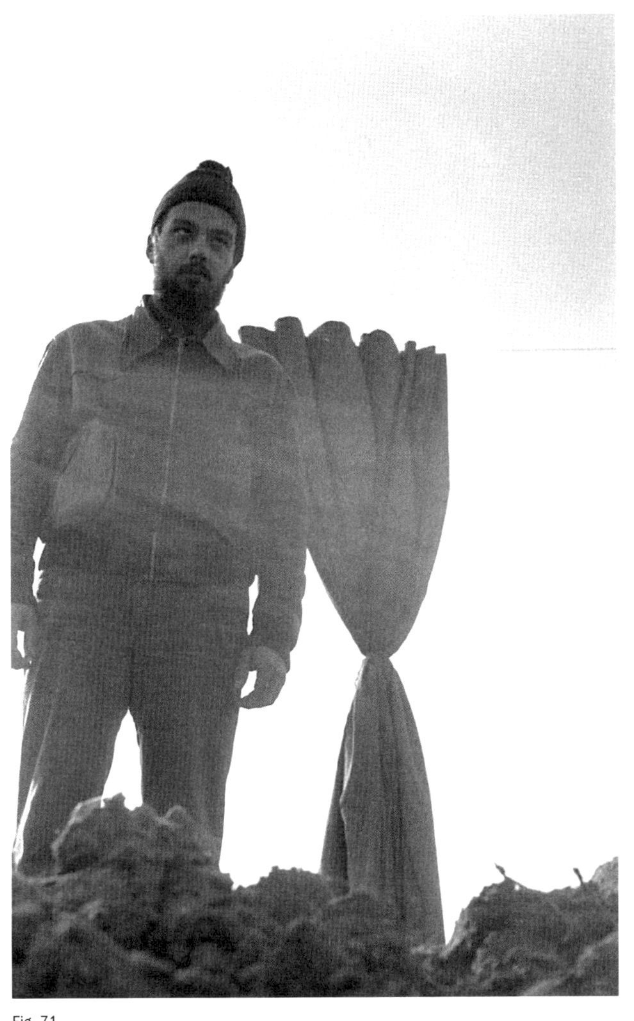

Fig. 71

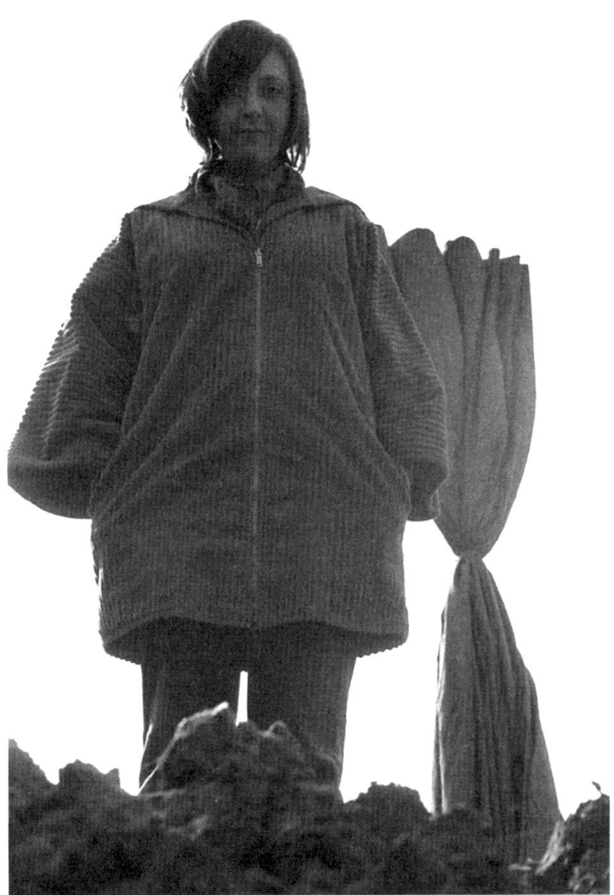

Fig. 72

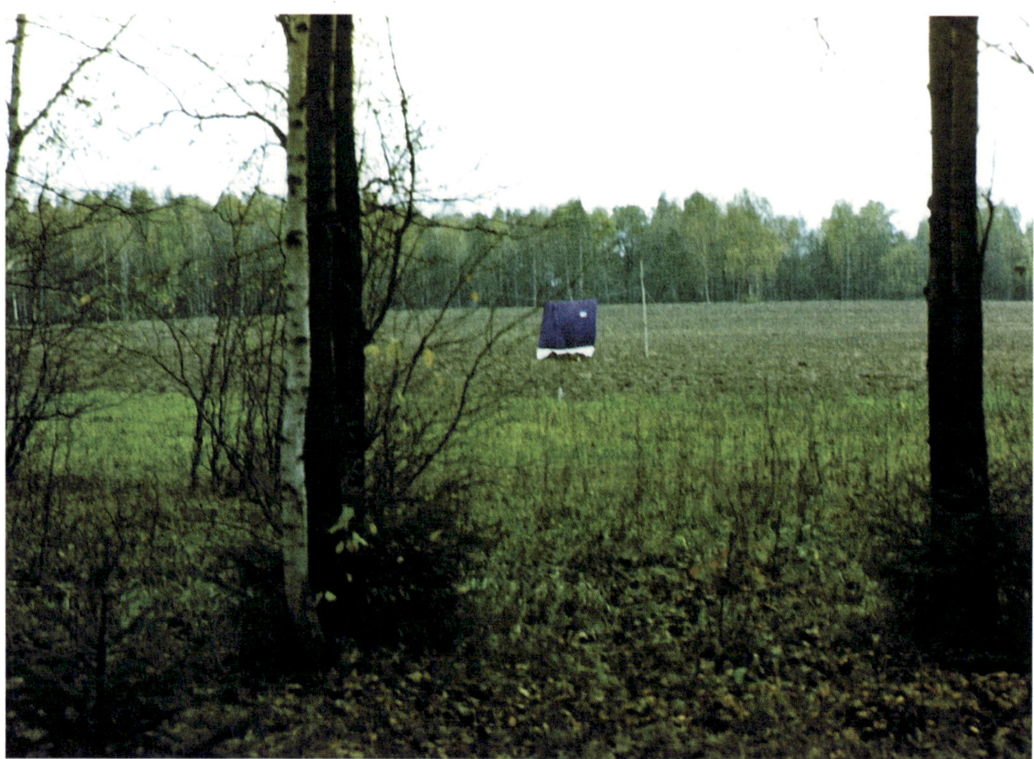

Fig. 73

away, physically liberating myself. In the ditch, another kind of spiritual process took over, the conscious and the subconscious were working. There was nothing else that had to be done there—I had already come on my own two feet to where I was supposed to be, and now what remained was for some of my other organs to take charge.

What is interesting is that this event felt like an impression of life, like an experience of a strange event, not like an impression of a work of art.

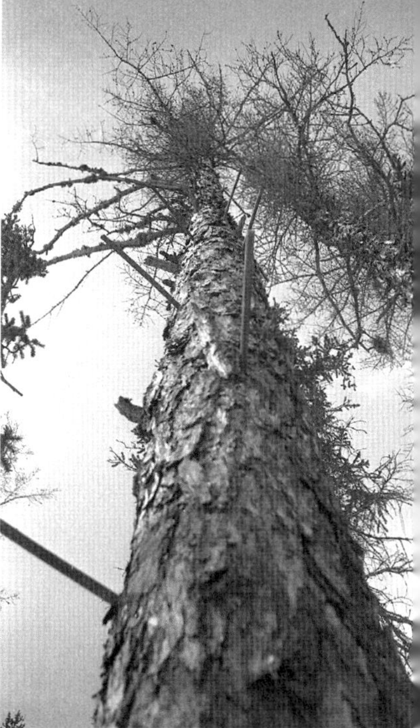

Fig. 74

Kiesewalter's Story: *For G. Kiesewalter*

George Kiesewalter, April 3, 1980

Around the middle of March, I received a letter with a proposal to independently carry out the next thing in the series of our "individual" actions; it was indicated that this one was designed expressly for the conditions and specifics of my Yakutian life.[27] The first accompanying letter was already included in the envelope. I was naturally happy about this invitation and began to wait for the package. From the contents of the first letter, I surmised that I would have to hang or set up either a slogan like the works of 1977–78 or some kind of soft construction on the edge of a field.[28] My conjectures were in large part based on the volumetric possibilities of a package, since what else can be sent through the mail, be suitable to long-range viewing, as stipulated in Point 4 (of the first accompanying letter), but not be cumbersome or heavy? Soon, from a telephone conversation with A.M., I learned that I would have to climb up several trees, so my suspicions were partly confirmed, and A.M. suggested that I find a suitable pair of trees ahead of time.[29] Having found a field of the required diameter outside the city and inspected the trees growing along its edge, I discovered that it would be practically impossible to climb up almost any one of them. The tall trees of the region have, as a rule, a tall canopy with a nearly bare trunk, so the branches begin to grow only at a height of six or seven meters above the ground. Thus, before the package arrived, I had to solve a technical problem: how to get into the tree and secure myself in it for the work that awaited. A solution was soon found: metal spikes around 30 centimeters in length were prepared on my specifications at the local factory. While they

27. At the time, Kiesewalter was living and working as an English teacher in the industrial town of Mirnyi in the far northeastern Soviet republic of Yakutia.
28. See Collective Actions works *Slogan-1977* and *Slogan-1978*, in which banners resembling official Soviet propaganda slogans were hung in the countryside.
29. Monastyrski is sometimes referred to as A.M.

were being made, I received the package with two more accompanying letters and sent a telegram confirming my readiness. The package was soft to the touch and all one piece, so I assumed definitively that it was some kind of slogan. On April 12, I set out with all of the equipment, including the package, letters, camera, hammer, spikes, and so forth. At the edge of the forest, I found the trees I had selected, 25 meters apart, and began to hammer the spikes into their trunks. At this point it became clear that I could only hammer while standing on the ground. When I tried climbing onto the ones already hammered in and holding the hammer in one hand and the next spike in the other, I could not maintain my balance to work—either a belt or a rope would have been necessary. On top of this, the weather suddenly worsened, and it began to snow. I decided to return later and left the backpack with all the things in it in the forest beneath the snow. My mood, of course, was ruined, all the more so since I had gotten tired and wet; I had had to work knee-, if not waist-deep, in the snow. On the following day, April

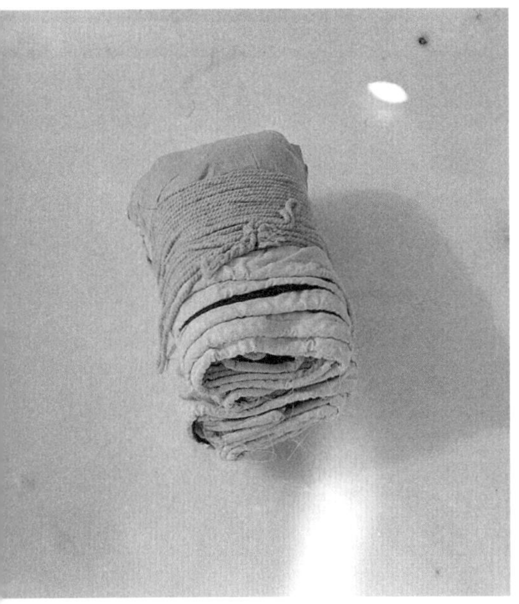

Fig. 75

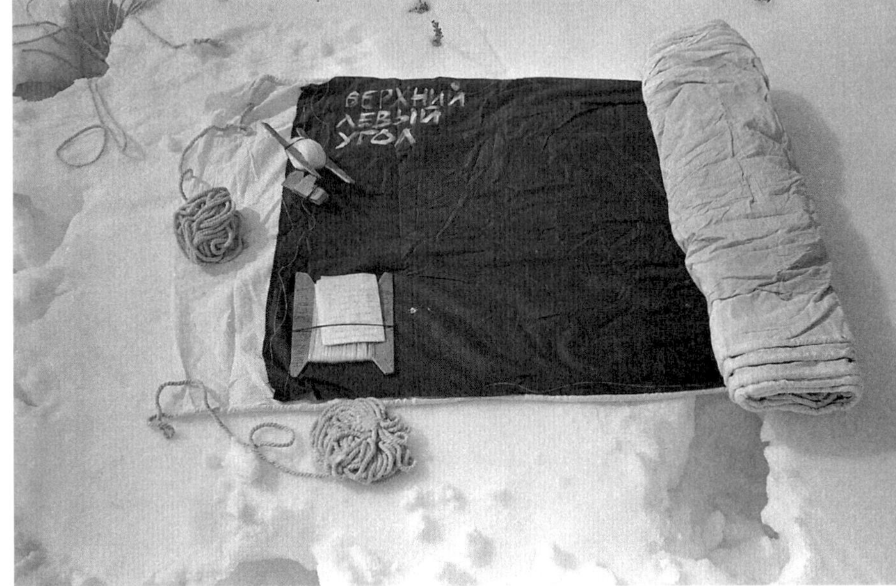

Fig. 76

13, I grabbed a solidly durable rope and set out once again for the field. This time I managed, though even with the rope tied around my waist and the tree trunk, the work was very difficult. Having climbed up in this way to a height of six meters or more, I opened the package and read the second letter. The package did indeed contain a slogan, whose text was covered by a black cloth, which was sewn using fishing line along the edges and the fishing line wound onto four bobbins. (I had been warned ahead of time that I should handle the package carefully and not damage any of the fishing lines—which is why at first I began to imagine some kind of light-weight, web-like construction that I would have to hang in the forest.) Now I was to hang this slogan on my own, evenly and symmetrically, not to mention that the weight of the damp fabric was now considerable and the gusts of wind were at times fairly strong. More than anything, I feared, along with the "makers" (the package contained a mass of instructions, pieces of advice, and recommendations) that the black sheet would fall off during the hanging and the goal of the action would not be realized. However, everything came off successfully even without any kind of advance planning or calculations. The slogan hung quite evenly and beautifully. But when I began to pull out the vertical fishing line, the right one got caught on something and crumpled the entire edge, so that I had to remove the whole right wing, take out the fishing line, and hang the slogan all over again. With this, the right edge of the black cloth peeled back, revealing the red letters at the end of the slogan. But to deduce which words these letters belonged to was impossible, and I did not even try. It was getting late, and I still had the journey through the "virgin field" ahead of me. Taking everything with me and unwinding the two bobbins simultaneously, I walked away into the field the entire distance of the fishing lines (130 meters). I thus had to cross this distance of deep snow three times. At the final position, standing in the field before the slogan, I read the third letter. The tiredness and even irritation that had built up after all my troubles were replaced by surprise, a kind of cathartic laughter, understanding, and agreement. Following the instructions, I pulled out the fishing lines, moving in line with the bobbins to the

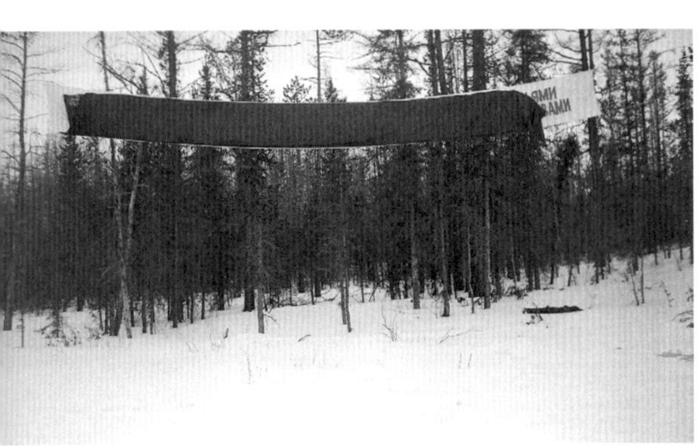

Fig. 77

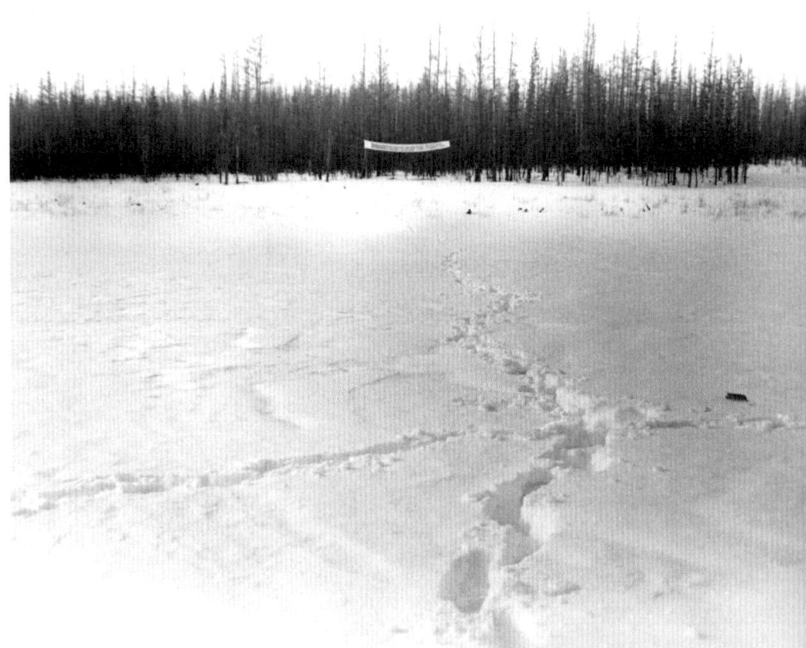

Fig. 78

left and to the right of my position. Here everything went smoothly, despite the distance. All I had left was to photograph the unveiled slogan and leave it there, never having learned its message. However, looking at the slogan through the viewfinder, I suddenly realized that I could, if I wished, make out the text even at this distance! The temptation, of course, was great, but I had managed to defeat it earlier, upon receiving the package and letters, while hanging the slogan, etc. And so, in order not to ruin the idea of the piece in which my vision had not been taken into account, I simply tried not to look too closely at the slogan, took several photographs, and left.

Kabakov's Story: *Ten Appearances*

Ilya Kabakov, February 8, 1981

I will now try to remember the impression that I had during the action last Sunday. It was stipulated ahead of time that anyone who went would be participating in the action. And moreover, it was also specified that the presence of anyone not participating in the event was not desirable. Thus from the outset, this unconsciously created a kind of esoteric and closed situation, considering that we usually go to C.A. actions with those closest to us, and so they have always had a free, unfettered presence to them. But now, these strict conditions seemed to create a cut-off, severed circle from the rest of life. Thus, a certain preliminary participation seemed already present in our impressions and experiences, and it seemed to accompany us on our ride and in our anticipation of what was to take place. And so it is this cut-off feeling that I would like to highlight.

We found ourselves on that same field where I had been several times before. Leaving the road behind, we were immediately plunged into deep snow and had to walk in step. This physical hardship of stepping with legs not very fit for the task and without the help of skis into deep holes, into these tunnels cut deep into the snow, immediately focused the mind on this heaviness and hardship.

Nevertheless, we found ourselves at the very center of the field, at a large and even distance from the surrounding forests. The organizers were already gravitating toward and circling something, and we approached it as partici-pants. It was a flat board with rounded edges, and it had ten nails driven into it with bobbins of string attached. The participants were unwinding, fastening, and testing the strings. Soon we were given the assignment to walk radially, like stars, like rays, from the center, while holding in our hands the strings that we had been given. We each wound them on our hands for strength. When I began to look around to my left and right, getting ready for the signal that would indicate that I could move, I saw everyone in the same comical pose. Everyone was waiting like animals at the starting line, readying themselves for the start of the journey. I dwell on this because it has deposited itself in my memory as a kind of pre-anticipation of the beginning, of the launch. And then we were off. Each one of us went in our own direction, following the faint marks in the snow leading us toward a different section of the forest's edge. I no longer looked around, but only moved, trying to walk in a straight line. I was immediately overtaken by an even stronger state of heaviness and physical fatigue, since I no longer walked

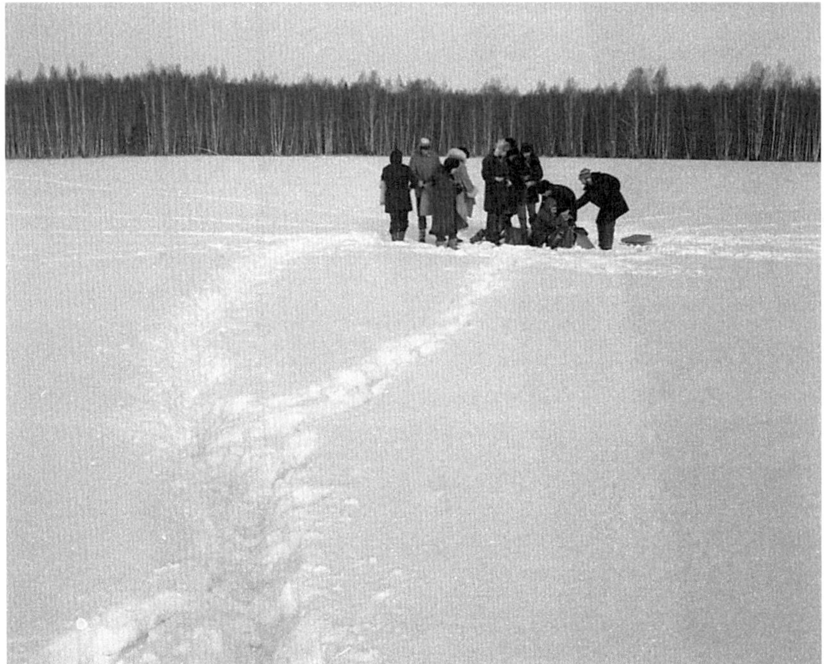

Fig. 79

in someone else's steps, but through virgin snow. Even though the weather was good and the mood excellent, this dragging of the legs through the snow did not so much sap the strength as it created a hardship that drove all outside thoughts from the mind and spirit. The difficulty lay not in trying to keep from falling, but in the frustration and burden of stepping in this endlessly deep snow, of sinking in each time above the knee.

Still, slowly but surely, anticipating when this sinking through the snow would finally end, I neared the forest. I repeat that because of this physical hardship, there were no other feelings or impressions. Finally, after some difficulty and dreariness, I reached the edge and was absorbed into the forest. I passed several fir trees and turned around. And indeed, as had been predicted, the field was no longer visible from here. I stopped in this wondrous forest like Ivan Susanin among completely untouched, snow-covered firs, tree trunks, and so forth.[30] Then, I turned and began to pull the string, which had landed on a branch about four or five meters away. I saw it shimmering like a ray against the snow, and this ray shone in the beautiful, sunny day. All in all, everything was fairly idyllic—light blue and rose-colored—and I continued to pull the string, winding it onto my right mitt. It wound and wound, but since I was trying to understand what lay ahead, what trick I was supposed to discover and what the whole idea was about anyway, it was as though my imagination was also winding with it, as though this winding was also the time of my standing in the forest. As long as I am winding, so long will I continue to stand. Because I am winding, so I am standing. I will keep standing so long as I continue to wind the string. Curiously, my feelings gradually began to shift: I stand as long as I am winding, but on the other hand, I wind as long as I am standing. This "figure-eight" began to oscillate and pass over from winding to standing. But I should say that I experienced no liberation or prostration, because I was concerned the entire time with how long I would have to stand there. For one thing, it was cold. Then I began to suspect the organizers of a certain excruciation, or rather, of involving me in a fairly unpleasant situation. I remembered that there had been a previous action where people pulled

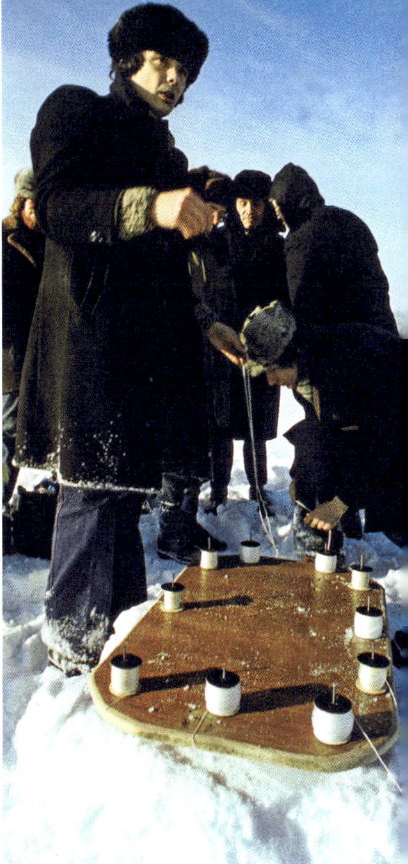

Fig. 80

30. Ivan Susanin, Russian folk hero and subject of an opera by Mikhail Glinka. His name is now associated with somebody who claims to know the way while leading his followers deeper and deeper into confusion.

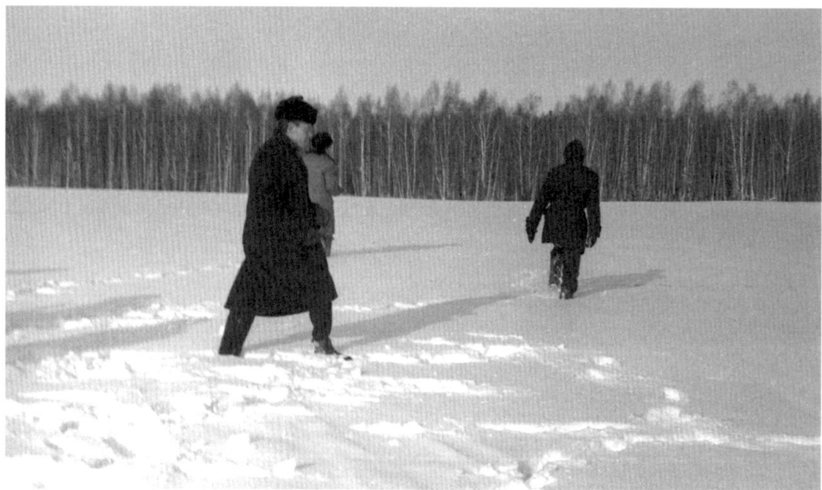

Fig. 81

a rope out of the forest for an hour and a half. It lay in an enormous pile on the ground, but still had to be pulled and pulled. I began to fear that perhaps they had attached some more string onto this one (since I had seen the bobbin and there was not that much there), and now I feared that they had wound on an entire cable drum that had been smuggled in someone's briefcase. I remembered that Andrei had something heavy rolled up in his briefcase, and I became afraid, because I was not prepared to stand in the snow for an hour and a half, all the more so because I had already grasped everything and the exalted prostration was not setting in. My fear increased when I began to watch for knots in the string and looked in horror when a knot with additional string did actually appear. But then after a while, I felt the tension on the string grow slacker, and suddenly, I remember, I could see the tension of the string weaken and the length shorten in my hand. And then suddenly, I saw something that looked like a little marble appear on the branch that I had been watching, along which that little ray of string had been gliding, and this was the end of the string. I had never in my life experienced anything as incredibly gratifying and joyful as this. I had been alone, and then at the end of this event of mine, there appeared a sign, a gift, and even a message in the mystical sense. Now I was truly overcome by some mystical melancholy and a feeling that I was about to learn something. I should say that this was not simple curiosity, but a completely irrational state. I even started to prolong it. I did not pull the marble to myself immediately, but instead started to watch as it bounced, making its unhurried passage through the snow from dip to dip. It was a sensation very similar to *Sadko* or *The Snow Maiden*.[31] I dwell on this for a long time, because it was a very powerful and important experience. Finally, this marble or ring—I could not make out what it was, it had the character of a gift or a message—rolled up to my feet. I pulled it up from the ground and brought it closer to me. But still, I could not guess what it was; that is how unusual and like a fairy-tale this impression was. The object had completely dematerialized and floated in this mysterious fairy-tale gift. It seemed to glow in the midst of this solitude, this snow, this sun-filled day. At last, I unfolded the note and read. It should be said that since the event that was the "message" had already happened, what was written there in the note—what was concretely there and what were its true contents—did not really matter to me. The experience itself of what I have just described above had already happened. When I discovered that it contained the names of the organizers along with the date and place of the action, I not only had no reaction, but even thought, very well then, there was not supposed to be anything there in the first place, since thanks to this gift and message, the thing for which all of this had been done had already been achieved. This note, of course, was just the signature beneath the action indicating the end of the pulling and the end of the event. But what follows is curious: no further instructions from the organizers had been given.

And now, whatever else I was to do in no way followed from what had already taken place. I had a certain field of freedom and I had to decide what to do next. Admittedly, there was no doubt or hesitation as to what to do, to leave or anything like that. Immediately after this elation, I wanted to share my impressions and also to thank those who had created it for me. This was

31. *Sadko* and *The Snow Maiden*, Russian folk tales that take place in enchanted settings and on which Nikolai Rimsky-Korsakov based two of his most famous operas.

an instant and natural moment of return. I began to shuffle back. Naturally, I feared that the others might not share my desire to return, and would leave. But happily, when I came out of the forest, I saw a cluster of those same people in the distance. With incredible joy, practically leaping from hole to hole, I raced back, so pleased was I by everything that had happened to me. And this happy and joyful state lasted as I retraced my steps in the reverse direction, and it did not leave me once I had completed my return. Here is how I might analyze it. What was the meaning of this joy? In the midst of this return, there was an echo of that same unconscious impulse that flashed when we were all standing at the starting line at the beginning of our radial journeys. In other words, it was as though we had been released, directed somehow, our journey pre-programmed by those who had conceived all this. They had conceived ahead of time how I would feel after all these trials and perturbations: a kind of pleasant and cheerful, terribly harmless, play-ful and, I would even say, tender and touching kind of game or a toy that not only brought no harm, no mockery, but instead brought nothing but

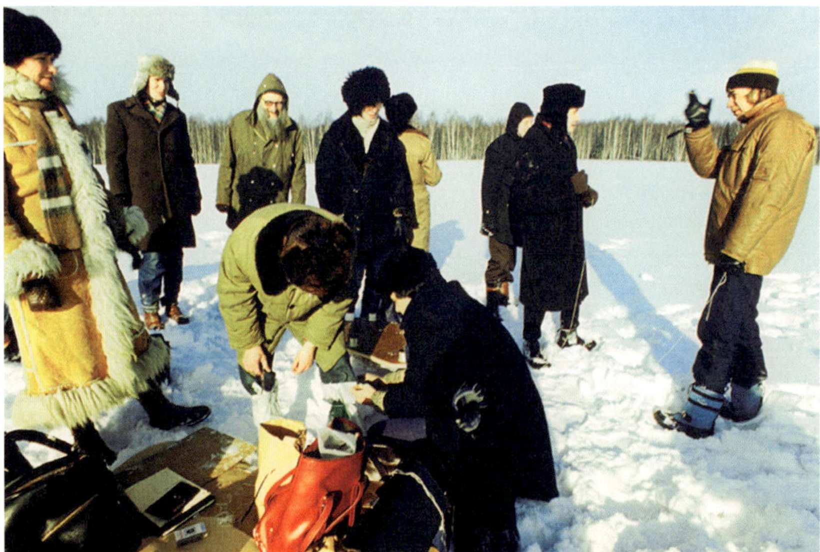

Fig. 82

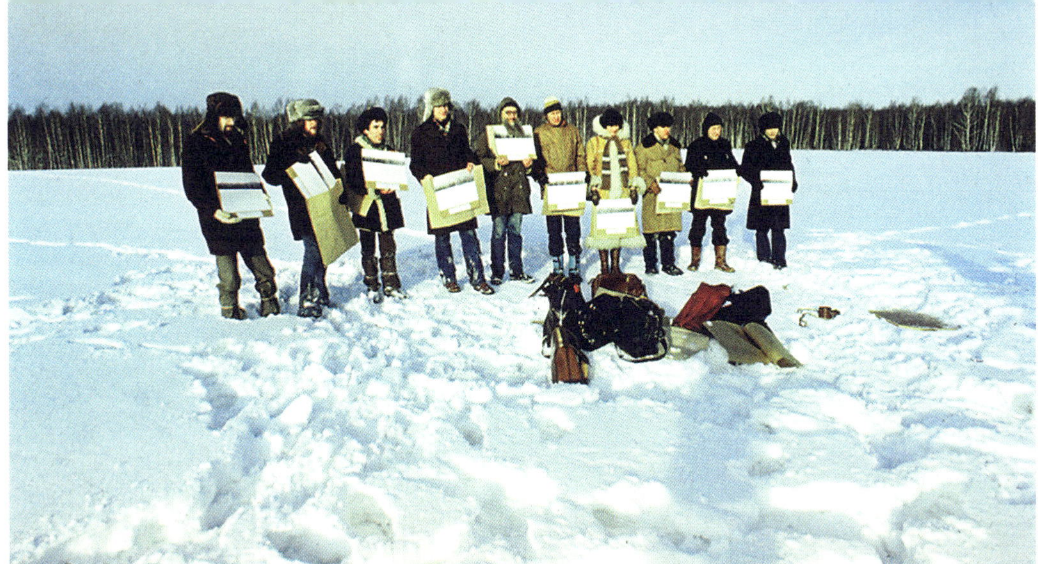

Fig. 83

delight. It is a familiar situation from childhood when playing, for example, hide-and-seek: someone devises a scheme, someone deals the slips of paper, somebody hides. But no ill follows: nobody boxed you in the ear, stuffed shit down your collar, or tripped you with a stick. On the contrary, it all concluded with much merriment and amusement. In other words, we are dealing with some kind of happy games, which, apart from goodness and unity, leave nothing behind. It is a feeling of unity with the friends who created this for you and those who returned. This pleasant feeling, finally, is what produced the entire meaning and desire to return to the participants and organizers. This is what, in fact, characterized the event.

I would like to observe three steps here. The first one is mysterious, when you are first sent off. This very much resembles a "game with friends." The second is the "solitary gift" itself. And the third is gratitude and the pleasant return into the bosom of the group. It should be said that here was achieved one of the most pleasant and practically unknown forms of society, which is today so agonizing. Here society does not appear hostile, but benign, vouchsafed and sympathetic to the highest degree. This is such an untried, unknown feeling, that it not only restores these lost forms, but itself seems to serve as a gift against the background of everything that exists today.

Nekrasov's Story: *Ten Appearances*
Vsevolod Nekrasov, February 1981

We can begin from the middle, or even from the end, from the moment when the little string was pulled out, and the little note found itself in the hand. The little note, it was simply a kind of appellation, not really a text, but the title of a text: *February 1981, Kievy Gorki, Moscow Region*. Why? Because the naturalism of the whole thing was simply too high. The authors somehow managed to gain mastery over all the things named in the little note and to declare them all their own creations, as if to say, please make a note of this. And indeed, there was nothing left to do but to note it. And truly, the work was a very successful one. Even the weather did its part, I think. Everything turned out very well. The trick is that all of it was very well directed. Everything fell into place, nothing got in the way, and each part only added to the whole. For example, you are pulling this little string, and the string is made up of different parts that pull in different ways: it gets stuck, it runs smoothly, it goes slack. I am no fisherman, or else I probably would have had some other sensations and associations of pulling something out of this horizontal space as out of the water. But even without the fishing, everything was somehow very good. The string would get matted, then wet when it would fall into already-melted snow, then get a piece of bark caught on it. I threw this bit of bark away mechanically and then thought, eh, it's a shame I did this, for this will all now wind up in a ball, into another kind of space in which the whole day will be preserved with signature and stamp. But some little piece of bark remained in there; the string did not wind on just anything, but on some little branches that had broken off. I decided to continue winding it onto them.

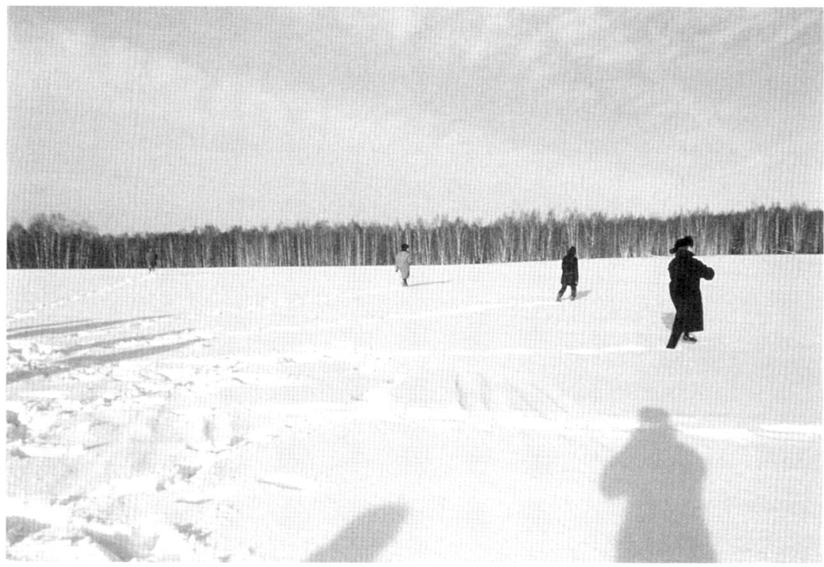

Fig. 84

I have to also say something about the working out and elaboration of this space. It took place along a radius, like on the metro map of Moscow—from one point and in all directions. Too bad there was no helicopter, or else Makarevich's best photo would have been a bird's-eye view of all of these divergent tracks, well-lit by the sun. This would have been great. But no matter. That was just it: there was a minimum of technology, no helicopter, not even skis. Everything was reduced to the most basic things, and with good reason. It makes sense why there weren't skis. Where's the interest in that? And even just visually, graphically, we would have ruined, trampled on, and marked up the entire field. And then the tracks would have lost their meaning. But here, each step was taken seriously. You had to concentrate— you would not jump an extra step in this snow. You had to choose your steps carefully and, where possible, in a straight line. It is very amusing to turn back and see that where you thought you were walking straight turned out not straight at all. Only the little string draws out perfectly straight, stretches out into a straight line, while you, for some reason, always walk crookedly, from side to side, even when this is not in your best interests. And then, of course, this little string was very beautiful in the forest.

In other words, this whole situation was very playful, magical, and artistic—and all of it was unified, like in a child's game that always has all of these things. All of this exists in object poetry, too. I am referring to what I was saying about authorship and the appropriation of the Moscow Region, Kievy Gorki, the day itself, of the entire piece, for which we can congratulate the organizers. Especially useful for this purpose was the little string, because it made everything very vivid, humorous, and interesting. If I had seen this string lying there all by itself, of course, I would not have contained myself, and if there were no one around, I would have pulled it, wondering, what is this little string? And, in general, if we were to stretch the string all the way across the field and then through the woods, how would it go? This is an interesting question. It was all somehow very natural and great, how it snagged on all the little curlicues, on every tree trunk on the road. It probably worked out even better for me than for somebody who had not come upon a road on his way. But I came upon a road in the forest, and it was fairly crooked. Imagine an axis that is straight, toward which the string gravitates, wishing to be straight in its movement. But all around it are these curves in the road. And the way that all of these deviations differ from one another—where it will get snagged, where it won't—all of this is very interesting. I was sure that I would never pull it out in one piece, that this simply could not be. And yet, I did pull it out. It would be interesting to find out how many meters of string there were, probably 200 or 300. It was probably equal to the distance from the center of the field to the edge of the forest. It turned into a kind of poetic object. It is probably the best of all their pieces that I know. Up to now, the piece that I can see most clearly is *Time of Action*, of which I was not a part. *Place of Action* was also good, but different somehow. In it, the act of dwelling in this world was different in the way it was felt and made sense of. In other words, this universal artistic problem was very strongly expressed there,

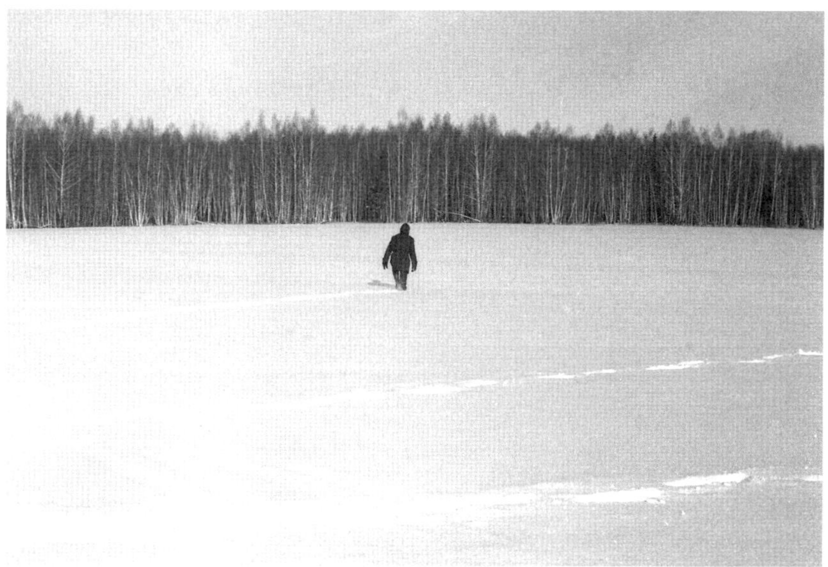

Fig. 85

but in slightly more diffuse terms. The constructive side was nearly absent, though it was surely meant to be this way. Or rather, it was overly detailed, which amounts to the same thing. There was no guiding thread for the whole thing to be found. Or perhaps, it had a different approach altogether, which was all very reasonable. But in any case, having this thread here made all of this particularly well felt.

Having pulled out and read the note, I took it as an ending, as "regards." As saying, there you go, comrades so-and-so are concluding this activity, of which they are informing you; they salute you, and wish you well on your way. And indeed, this path through the snow on foot had not been easy, as if to say, there would be no way back, taking into account the instruction to go into the forest until the field could no longer be seen. The point was to go in and then to act according to the circumstances. For me, it turned out that I came upon a road and wound my string perhaps not as energetically as expected, and thus, I walked so far that I no longer saw the field, but saw instead the other end of the forest. And since I was walking along a road, I thought that it probably followed that I should continue walking to this other end of the forest, that there would be something there. (You could already see some houses over there in the distance.) This is what I did. Getting distracted from the activity, I would think, how so, how could such a thing be? Then I thought, probably such a thing could be. Because I am walking along a road; the road has turned up exactly in the place where I was pointed, which probably means that I was directed to this road. And in addition, at one point, I saw the movement of a skier behind me. I decided not to inspect him very closely, thinking, Lord knows, what if they are worrying on my behalf, what if I am being watched? Maybe yes, maybe no. Or what if there is somebody waiting up ahead? Or, what if there is nobody waiting for me, precisely because I am walking along a road and toward some buildings? In this case, it must be the other people who are being watched, because their paths are wilder and more blind. Here is how I figured it: there are 10 directions, three or four of which simply lead to the main road. This means that five, six, seven people can be counted on, and then there are enough roads like mine in different parts of the forest (I remember from the fall that there were many dirt roads in there). And since, say, Panitkov is missing, it is conceivable that he and perhaps another person are waiting to meet someone out there. In other words, it was all planned so that you would not have to return. And in any case, the basic idea was to act according to the circumstances. Mine turned out to be such that it was easier to move forward than to go back. And although there was just as much snow in front of me as behind, I could also see a road laid down by tractors up ahead. And so it was as though I had been set upon this path, as if to say, you go along this road. I thought, if anyone is being awaited, it is not likely to be me. Because of this road, which had been seemingly prepared for me, for my departure, I was not likely to be awaited.

And what's more, I thought I had been dawdling too long, had been winding the string for too long a time, and had outlasted the person waiting, if indeed there had been someone. To make a long story short, once

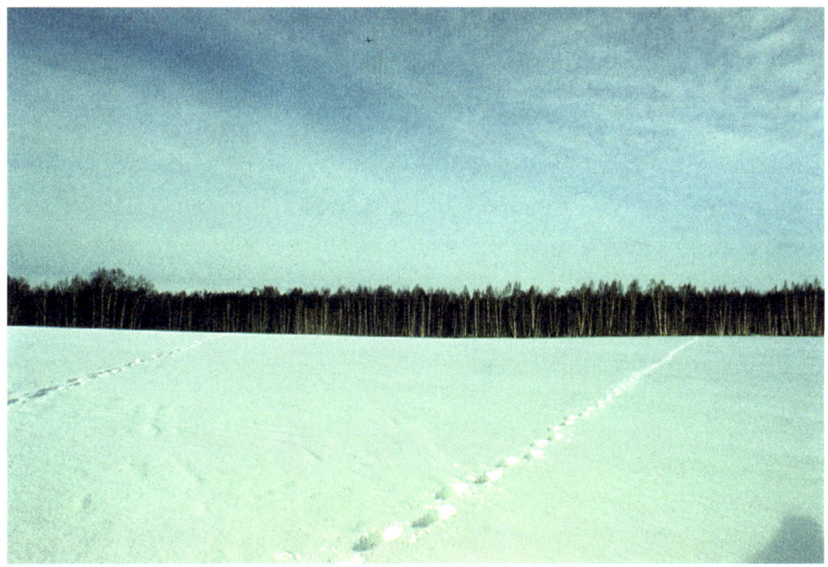

Fig. 86

I decided this, I went. And so, with some pleasure, I walked on, feeling some kind of natural enjoyment from this stroll, coming out of the forest and thinking, what is there, and there, and there? I remember thinking this must be the elaboration of space, according to Monastyrski, according to the original dispensation that he gave in the beginning when we were walking away from the little table with the bobbins. In other words: elaborate the space, comrades. Well, this, I think to myself, is very good. I seem to have been very well directed. I might as well elaborate it even more substantially, so I can continue walking and capture as large a section as possible. I seem to remember something in Lev Tolstoy about how much land a person needs. Well, if you are taking a section, then you might as well take a section. (Although truthfully, I was having a little trouble with a pain in my leg.) Nonetheless, as I was later informed, I had come out to the Institute of Feeds. Nobody told me that there was a commuter rail station nearby, or else I would have gone there. Instead, I got back on the road and then returned to the highway upon which we had come. I think I came out to the bus stop right before the one where we had exited. Maybe if the bus going in the direction of the field had come, I would have gone and spoiled the beauty and the wholeness of this work and come back out of simple everyday considerations: what if there were a group of people there? And anyway, I had made plans to see some of them. But there was no bus in that direction, and instead a bus came in the other direction, and on top of that, my leg was hurting, and I was certain that I had already outstayed everyone else, that I had walked too long, and that there could not be anyone else left. And so I calmly rode to Lobnya and got on the nearest commuter train, which was leaving in fifteen minutes. Some people could have come during that time, but nobody did. And anyway, I was sure that I was the last one. When I arrived in Moscow, as soon as I walked in the door, I got calls from Ilya and Oleg.[32] It turned out they had returned even later and had been waiting for me on the field. This had me somewhat confused. I thought about it once again, went over my reasoning, why I did not go back, and decided that I was probably not at fault, that if the responsibility belonged to anyone, it was probably to the organizers. Because the most important thing was to act naturally, according to the circumstances. I thought that there was a certain lack of ceremony, like in that joke: the old woman comes to the priest and says, you see, father, you go and go and go; and he says to her, you know, granny, do you see that door, so go, go, go . . . In other words, there was a certain lack of ceremony in this activity from the start, and after all, I had myself agreed to go. If at any moment, I felt something might be difficult, I could have easily turned and gone back—they probably would not have flogged me.

There was a balance there between real difficulty and symbolic difficulty. Or more precisely, the purpose of this difficulty seemed to have been calculated. The direction had been correctly set from the beginning, and the construction of the whole thing had been set precisely so that there could be no mistakes or blunders. This side of such activities is always fairly tricky. But then, I usually like these kinds of things, the ones with a certain guile.

32. Ilya Kabakov and Oleg Vassiliev (b.1931), artists and friends of Nekrasov who had participated in *Ten Appearances.*

All of this seemed to me no more unceremonious than, say, my own authorial unceremoniousness when I, for instance, begin to read a part of the text that has already been heard. In other words, this was familiar to me both in method and in a certain degree of mockery; I could see the possibilities in that. It would have been another thing, I think, for a person in a different mood, or if there had been different weather: this could have easily offended. Although who knows, and the way it turned out, turned out well. And then I found out that there was no mockery there to begin with. The return had been assumed all along.

If we consider a return, then it is, I think, a separate action in itself. It is something else, something separate, and even set paradoxically in contrast to the first part as something destructive and unexpected. And this destruction of the first part by the return is polemical. In the first part, everything is very finished, because of this idea of difficulty, and of the note that is torn—Zhigalov put it very well, like an umbilical cord is torn—once the note arrives.[33] The note is not instructive; it is a full stop. I think that this

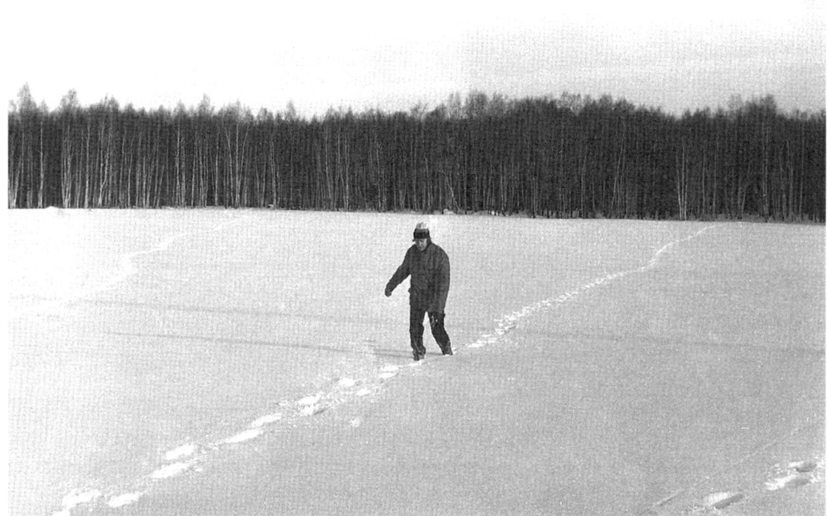

Fig. 87

33. Anatoly Zhigalov (b.1941), artist and regular participant in Collective Actions' activities.

move with the return is extra, it is conceived for creating a rigid presentation. Funniest of all in this sense was what happened when Zhigalov and I left. These false photographs of "appearances" turned out to be doubly false in our cases.[34]

There was also a nice graphic element, the texture of the tracks on the snow. You walk and see how beautifully, from the center out, these ten different tracks extend in ten different directions. You experience an aesthetic pleasure, begin to put in some effort, thinking, so what if it is difficult, and, good, that's the way it should be. Again, there is a balance of difficulty and attainability.

In other words, there is a natural difficulty here, which is at once toy-like and significant. There is a whole mass, a tangle of allegorical and symbolic meanings here that need not even be mentioned. It goes without saying: the string, the path—it's clear as day. But this is not particularly interesting. What is interesting is what grows out of it, i.e. real physical action, one that can be experienced aesthetically. One that can be experienced as pleasure, as a game. And not least of all because of the palpable graphic element of the journey in the snow. (Come to think of it, the fine weather could be considered a co-author here.) And then it is replaced by another graphic element, this time a concrete one. At first there was a traditional graphic element—the field like a sheet of paper—and then, I don't know how to put it, a more modern one, collage, assemblage, that is, how the little string moves.

And what, in essence, am I doing? I am describing my impressions of a very interesting and very pleasant walk. All walks could probably be described using such words, but you would not set out to describe every walk this way, nor should you. But in this case . . . You would not, after all, describe each little leaf or pebble, as the Japanese say. But all you have to do is to apply a frame around one, and there you have it: art. Well anyway, that is how it happened. The organizers applied this frame and many thanks to them for this, everything turned out fine.

I would like to repeat one more time that this, probably, is the most successful of all the things of theirs that I know. It is completely full-fledged. Any objections to this kind of art—that, say, it is too "artificial" or somehow

34. Nekrasov is referring to the doctored photographs of "appearances" that were presented to all of the participants, except Nekrasov and Zhigalov, upon their returns. See the full action description of *Ten Appearances*.

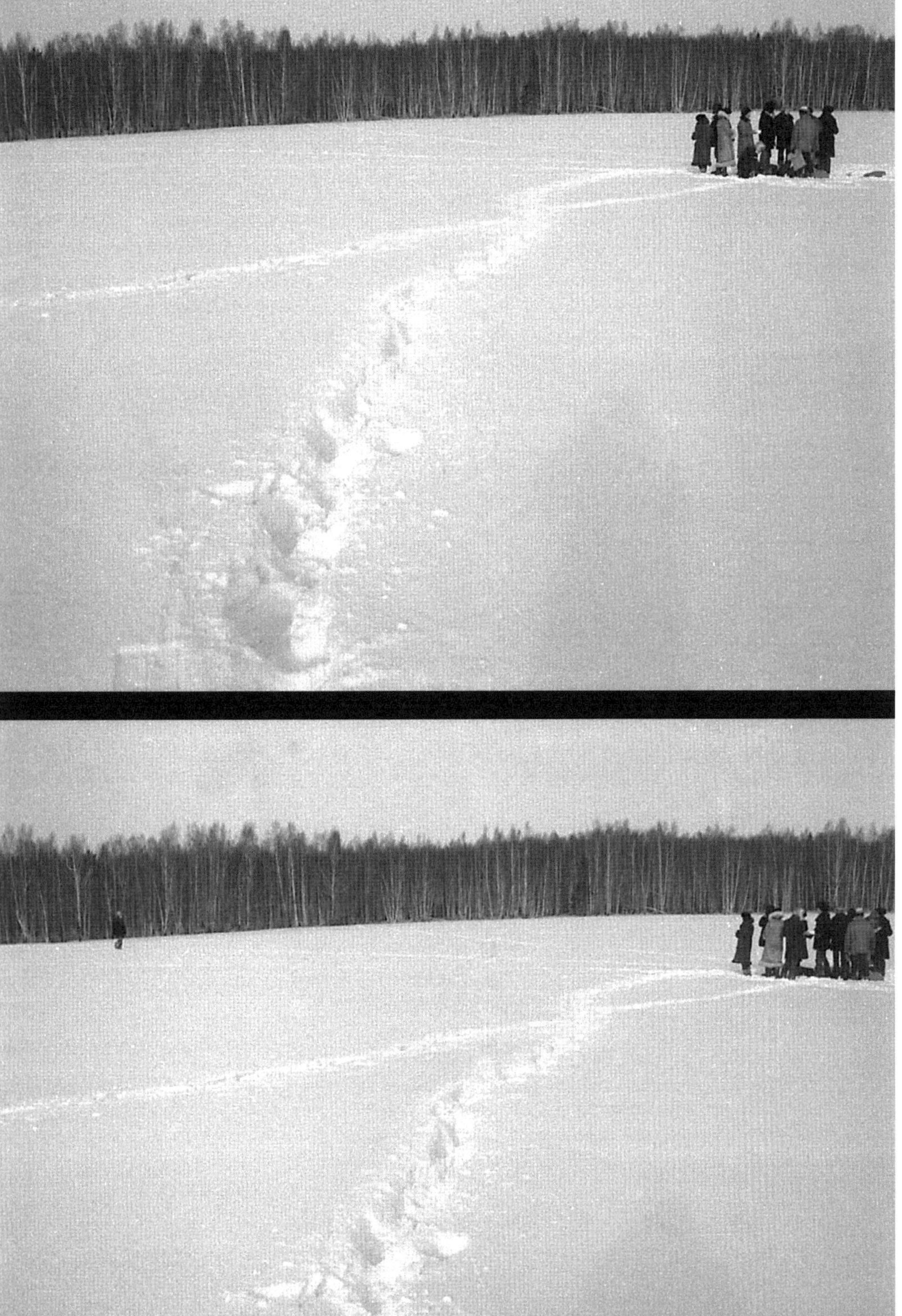

Fig. 88

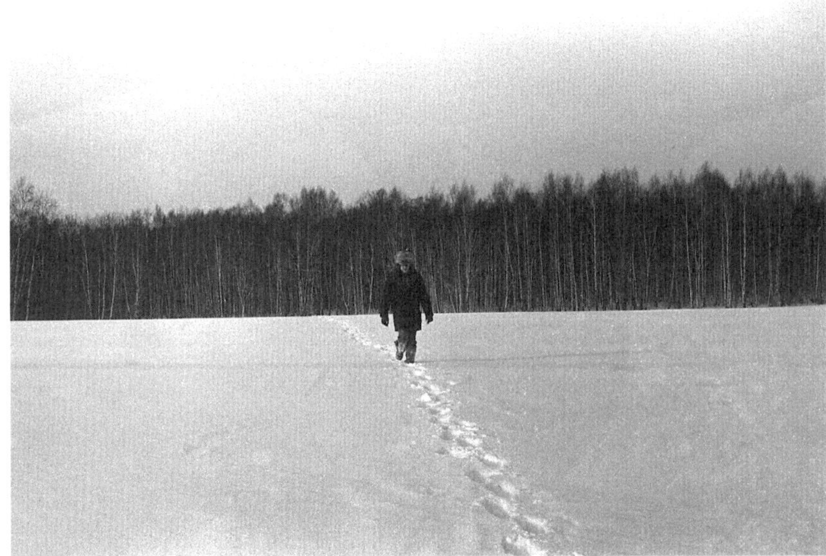

Fig. 89

defective—would not stand up here. Because it has everything that any normal lyrical work has, and has it through and through, as when an author has long ago identified himself with his method and everything lines up as it should.

There is another image here, a powerful one: the image of centrifugal motion, of the force that swings from the center circularly (and the circle itself, actually), and sends one out as far as possible, like Huck Finn with the dead rat on a string or like a hammer thrower. Actually, the end of the string, the one that had arrived with the little note, is not so much the umbilicus (I have never seen an umbilicus in my life), as a kind of tail trailing the movement, and also a little crack of a whip to spur you on, as if to say, hello, fly on farther.

Did you wind all the string up? Now wind yourself up and away.

The idea of appearances was nice, but I think that the main factor here, the main material of this thing, is still *relation*. Or to put it more literally, according to the organizers' prompts and stage directions, it is connection, the *connecting thread*. Relation and *non*-relation. How one turns into the other, in what way, by means of what other, new qualities.

At first it is a strange picture: 10 figures pick up the string ends and wander (on command, for some reason) in the directions indicated for them. Of course, at first, what is drawn tight is not just the little string, but the entire situation. It is not just dependence, but a single command: go! And so you go. But this is just the first moment; everything else begins on the second beat. You go and everything is interesting. And the farther you go, the more interesting it is. The interest is not in intrigue, in what you will find there (it is unlikely to be anything special). The interest is more interesting: you are yourself interested that you are walking, in how you are walking, in how the little string fares . . . While the little string is in the field and the tracks are in the snow, it is the purest graphic work on paper. In the forest, the little string is not the same as it is on the snow. It catches on the branches and trees. This is no longer graphic art, but something more avant-garde, forest-art, I don't know what, in any case, purest objecthood. And the relation comes into question: the clearing, the organizers, the bobbins—all are now out of sight.

The string was already wound (I wound it up myself onto whatever bobbin I had at hand). And here is the third level, the thread in a cocoon in my pocket. The thread is done, it no longer connects anything. The relation is concluded. Is that right? And now here is the most interesting part. From an artistic point of view, it is no longer graphic art, or any other kind of art, even with the most minimal materials and attributes. That is all, there are no longer any materials, and it seems that art has become not art at all. Even though in general, everything is the same, the shift is so natural and smooth that it is almost imperceptible. What we get, then, is something like a model of art's evolution toward a pure situational concept through a gradual, three-step process, an evolution from the point of view of the concept, naturally . . . Anyway, it is not that there is no material (such a thing is probably not possible), but that for me there is none, since I simply do not sense the material.

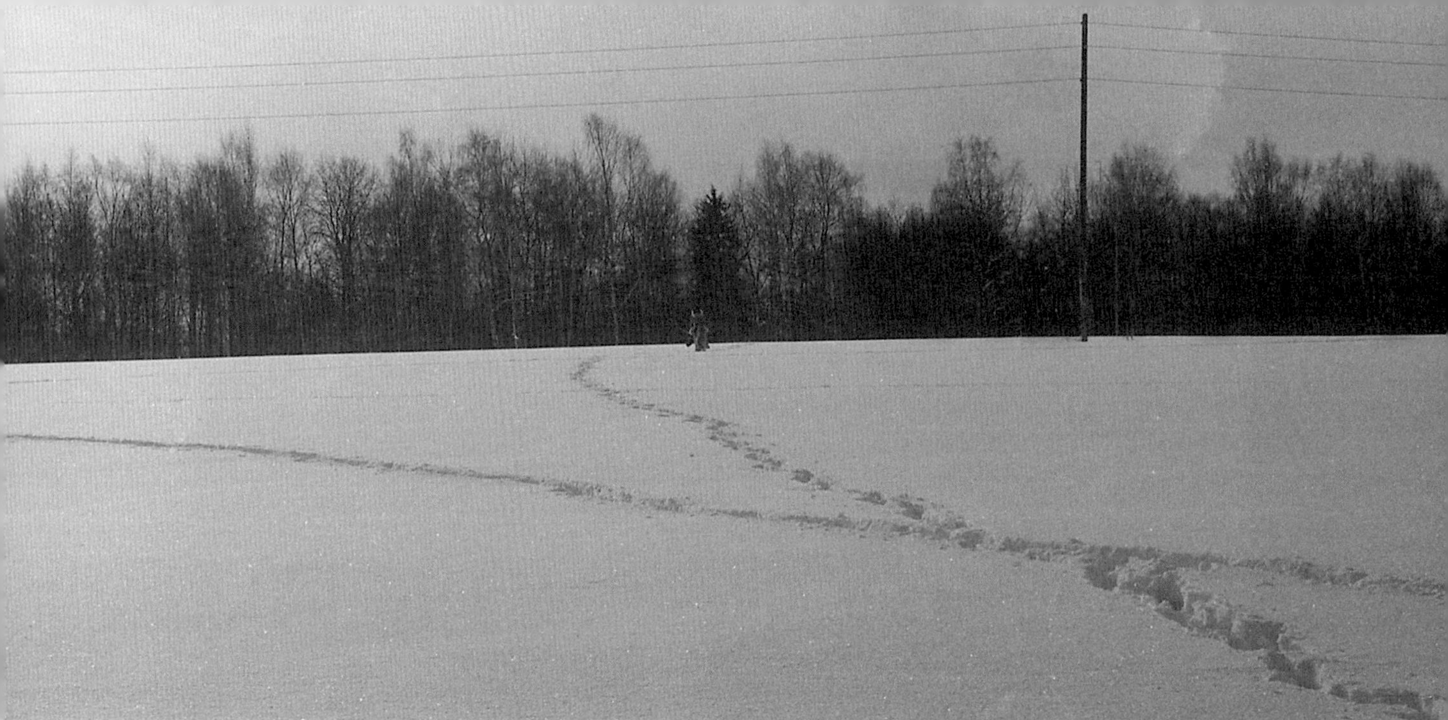

Fig. 90

Now I myself am the material. And the surrounding space, which I have been told to elaborate . . . And that the space is *way* out there where the houses are. They could have been a bit closer . . . And it turns out that it is even more *spacious* than one might like, rather . . . These relationships of ours with space, these normal games with problems of movement and space, which inspire us all to go on strolls and camping trips: these now serve as material for the organizers and for myself. The moment there—when the bobbin is no longer on their board, but in my pocket, the clearing is no longer visible, and the other edge of the forest is just coming into view—this point, in my opinion, is the peak of the entire thing, the high point of the concept. When I myself am the material itself, and the author and the organizer: therein lies the concept. "Oh dog, oh dog," says the dog to the dog, "do you know what a conditioned reflex is? Go and spit in the feed dish and you'll find out. That guy in the lab coat will come a-running." Now the organizers and us, we are holding each other by the tail even better than by the little nylon string, particularly when the tail of the string with the note ran up to you like a mouse in the snow. Incidentally, the note with the text could have probably contained our names, too, those of us who had been launched—and why not? Are we not also February, or Kievy Gorki, or this day, this weather, this place? How are we not also text, not also material? Because we now have it, the material, in a way? Well, in this way, they could be added too. We could be written in and added to the signatures . . . Because *correctly launched*, as the young members of the Moscow Art Theater used to yell, precisely launched. The strongest part of the concept, in my opinion, is its vectorness. It is aimed outward, naturally wants to become *all*, to get rid of the last remnants of the attributes of art, so that not even the root can be detected any longer (according to the famous antinomy of art/creation), to rise up into life, into reality, not just hypothetically—but in reality, exponentially . . . Above all, it is open to the real situation. All is right—it is a vector. The little string is there in order for a good launch, so that it tears with a satisfying ring; it is not there for pulling a piece of lard out of Kashtanka, I think.[35] In any case,

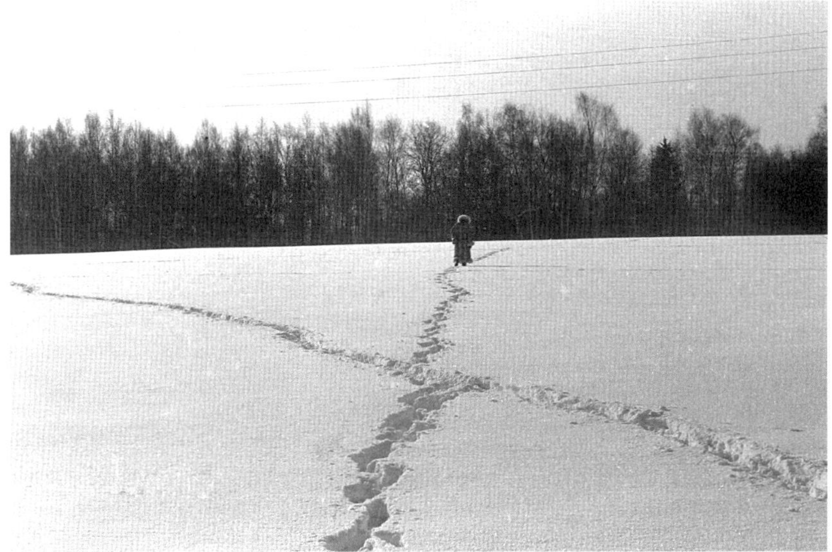

Fig. 91

35. Nekrasov is referring to an episode in Anton Chekhov's short story "Kashtanka" (1887), where Fediushka plays a trick on the dog Kashtanka by feeding her a piece of meat on a string and then pulling it back out of the dog.

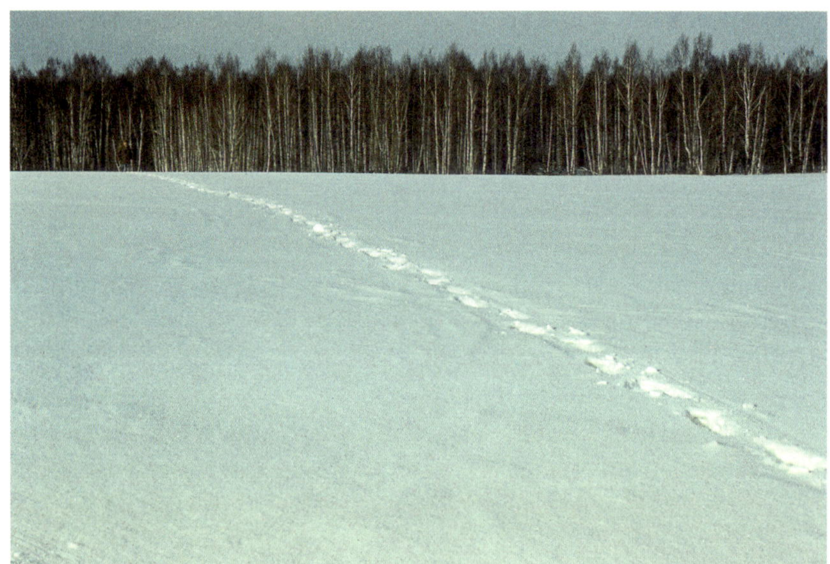

Fig. 92

on February 1, this vectorness was clearly in the foreground. From this view-point, you see that the most important aspect came out most strongly: the junction of action with the plane of the everyday. Or rather, not junction, you would not say junction, this is not so much a junction as the very knot itself. We are not speaking anymore about literal relation. I am outside relation, in non-relation; but I am *in the concept*. That's the thing of it. My 36 degrees of the terrain get wider, and that is how it should be, that is how it was con-ceived. The wider it gets, the farther you go, the better, it turns out—and this is the moment of the action's very breath—I carry out the goal of *elaborating space* (I can't remember, mastering . . .). And the freer I am, the more—how can I put it—armed (as Groys says).[37] And if I do not put on airs, then I will have to make use of this will of mine, having now made this detour by way of the Institute (as it later turned out) of Feeds named after Williams, a detour I would not repeat just for fun or exercise. This on the one hand. But on all the other, you find yourself ever farther away and in less comfort.

36. Boris Groys (b. 1947), philosopher and art critic active in Leningrad and Moscow in the 1970s, and one of the first writers on Moscow Conceptualist art.

And again, everything follows the construction's own axis, the launch route, creating a complete unity of the idea and the everyday reality of the situation. It is impossible to know now where the idea ends, when I will, so to speak, elaborate the entire space, each corner of the world that I am meant to. Is this how I should understand this? The action ended long ago, and yet the suspicion that it will never cease only grows. Sholem Aleichem asks, How does a boot-maker resemble a person? And his answer is that the boot-maker dies one day and so does the person. The concept tends toward universality and infinity, and all art tends toward the very same thing. It's just that the concept manages this not so much better—nobody is better, everyone is better—but *more vividly*.

It is like the hierarchy of degrees: subordination, coordination, predication[37] . . . And as predication faded away, I was launched. Precisely launched: although I am the one who walks, no longer playing but only wanting to get home, I am doing as intended. I can feel it myself, I don't know how to put it—nevertheless or all the more so . . .

And why did I not return? It was with full sincerity that I did not. All of the steps turned out to have been calculated in ideal proportion to pull me out to the Institute of Feeds, and moreover, calculated for unidirectional movement, for vectorness. At first, it was closer to the other edge of the forest than to the field behind. And even earlier, from the edge of the field, it seemed that it was closer to this *point*—Point A, let's say—than back to the center of the field. The other edge of the forest is then Point B. From there you can see that it is closer to the more or less well-trodden road than to the field.

On the road—at, let's say, Point C—you can see that the real road is already right there, no more than half a kilometer away.

And there, of course, is Point D, when you discover that this road does not go where you need it to. But to return (in the snow) is simply unthinkable. You've already cleaned your coat tails and shaken out your boots . . . If you had only known it earlier . . . Just like in real life, in other words. And it is always thus.

37. Nekrasov is referring to three types of syntactical relations.

There is, of course, also a bit of torment here, but the question is: whose is it? Is it not my own, since we have all gathered here together, we conceptualists?

And also, there is perfect unity even from the point of view of the seemingly long-surpassed aesthetic angle. Why ruin that graphic element?

Makarevich in a helicopter would not photograph the kind of rumpled, double trace that I describe. It would not be striking. And again, I am like a pencil, a drawing instrument. I find myself here simply with my own experience. To go back over one's own tracks is not only tiresome, but also just more difficult than walking through virgin snow. Snow begins to tramp down only on the third time maybe, but not after the first walk-through. No matter whether by foot or on skis. You can quarrel with this, but this is my opinion, and it was mine to walk. So, better not to walk, though the return is always there in principle. (I imagine how Misha Sokovnin would put it: the whole *intonation of the situation*—pure *Varius*.)[38] But simply everything, the whole steely construction, the whole orientation of it: everything was done so that return will be absurd, and simultaneously so from every point of view (the real one and every other one). And then there comes a moment when the construction might seem suspect, precisely in its redundancy— what is it for? Might there not be a trap here? If everything pushes you in one direction, does nothing but repeat in one voice "obey, obey," then maybe all is not so simple. This is where you might think: should I really obey? This might be the most interesting and the most content-filled moment of the whole undertaking. The moment when the allegorical, conceptual plan (the path, the thread, etc.)—both self-evident and inserted from the get-go, and therefore requiring not only conversation, but comprehension— announces itself, and in such a way that it turns on the central, conceptual problem, the one requiring activity, the one that I must now solve.

So how, finally, should this conception be understood? This *undertaking* of the architects, you understand, who have appropriated all of the surrounding space which I am now *elaborating*, and the entire situation, and myself within the situation, as their own text. Should we understand it as

38. Mikhail Sokovnin (1938–1975), underground Russian poet and writer. Nekrasov refers here to the work *Kniga Varius*, co-authored by Sokovnin and artist Aleksandr Malkov.

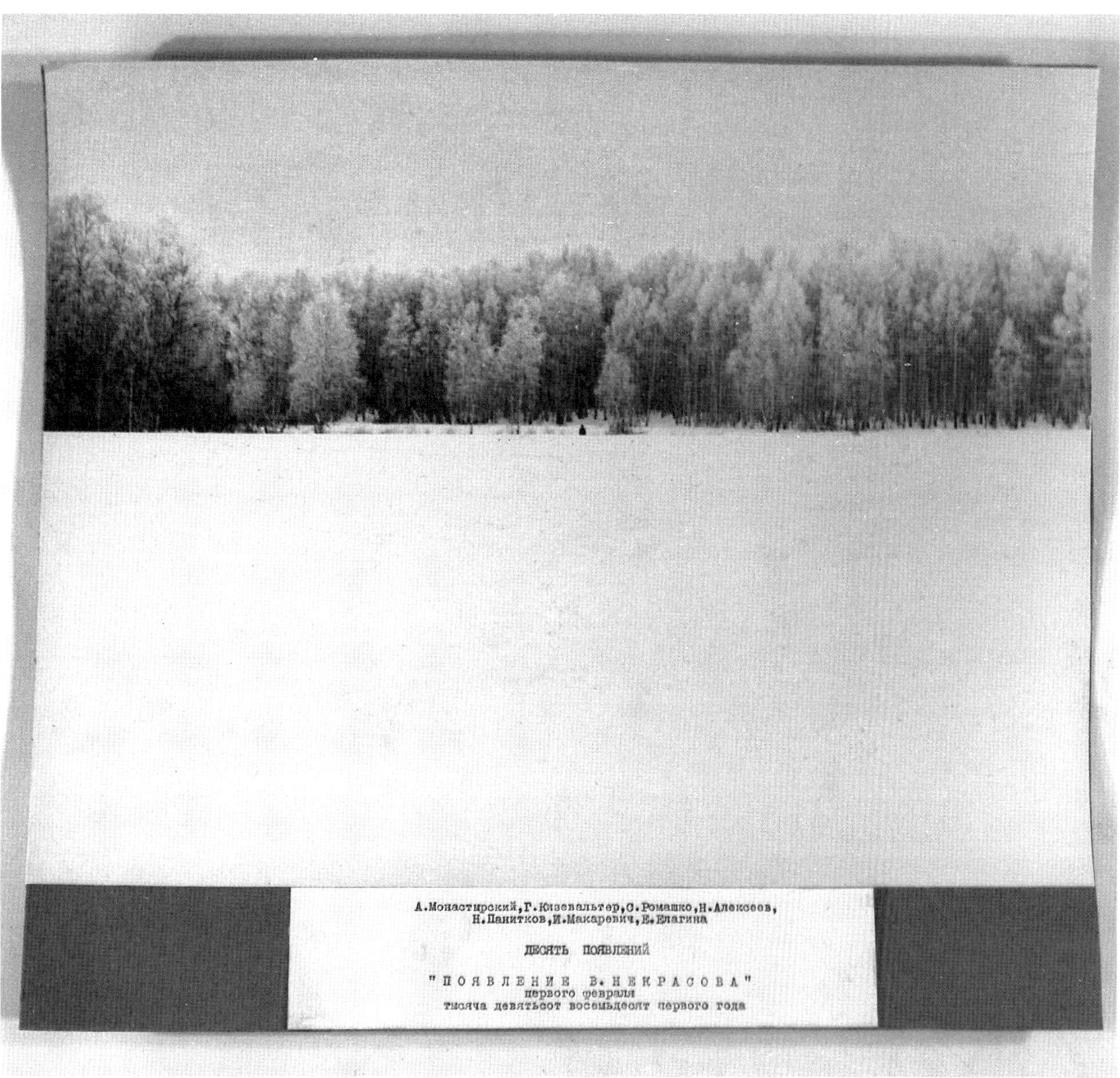

А.Монастырский, Г.Кизевальтер, С.Ромашко, Н.Алексеев,
Н.Панитков, И.Макаревич, Е.Елагина

ДЕСЯТЬ ПОЯВЛЕНИЙ

"ПОЯВЛЕНИЕ В.НЕКРАСОВА"
первого февраля
тысяча девятьсот восемьдесят первого года

Fig. 93

a *benevolent* undertaking or what . . . ? Benevolent or malevolent? After all, it is not for naught that somebody gave it the title, "Delusion and Disarray." Or, one's own Ivan Susanin. It is very similar to the following situation: we will all get together, scatter in different directions, and just you watch, you yourselves will no longer want to return here and gather together, even though an hour or two ago you did not even consider any of this . . . But here is where my will appears: oh, so this is how it is, well then, I will go back on purpose. Big deal . . . Fancying themselves fate . . . Yes, but when you think about dragging yourself through the snow . . . Well, let's say that I could do it if I had to actually return . . . But what does it mean "had to," for whom is this "had to"? But actually, it is a clear, pure, poetic-narrative instance, a perfect instance—why not revolt? So then the return is expected . . . But incidentally, there was also a return in Hiawatha. There was also a poetic instance there . . . Oh, I could spit on all of these contrivances. I made a plan with Oleg and Ilya, asked Ira Pivovarova to take some poems . . . Stop, this cannot change anything, it is all envisioned in advance, pre-programmed, and should be factored out from the beginning. Even up to now, I was not walking farther away because I had planned to walk farther, I was not playing around in any way, which means that everything is still the same, and now, most likely, there is no one left, or else it would not all have been like this, it would have been different.

In a word, the plan of the *action* and the plan of *reality* turned out to balance and merge. Everything was so constructed at every step that the only conclusion you could have was: you could return of course, in principle, but this would clearly be on purpose and somehow insincere. This suddenly illuminated, narrative-lyrical layer is far more alive this way, in its potentiality, than in any real, clumsy return. There, it would be compromised in its deliberateness and would itself come out obtrusive, contrived, and artificial. In a word, life resembles a plot. (And by the way, might we adopt this term, plot?) You wouldn't leap out of a plot, and you wouldn't leap out of life, if the plot is launched correctly. What we get is life-art; that is how we should understand it. And here is what I think. It turned out so cleanly in the end precisely thanks to the vector, thanks to the fact that the plot was unidirectional. It does not work in the reverse direction of return. Does it even make sense to demand that it work that way? Let this simple, everyday, technical, organizational—in a word, dull—moment remain here. It is, I think, outside the scope of things. That is, the return is *outside the plot.* And the "appearance" with the photographs, in its way, is probably a separate, a whole other plot after all, a plot that uses, cultivates the tail end of this outside moment. Though the plot is also engaging in itself, especially and most likely when applied to those who did not re-appear . . .

(The first part, the "story" itself, was transcribed from a tape recording. The second part was retyped from a hand-written manuscript.)

Appearance

The viewers were sent invitations to the action *Appearance*. Five minutes after the guests (30 people) had gathered and arranged themselves at the edge of the field, two of the action's participants appeared from the forest on the opposite edge. They crossed the field, approached the viewers, and presented them with certificates ("Documentary Evidence") attesting to their presence at *Appearance*.

March 13, 1976
Moscow, Izmailovsky Field
A. Monastyrski, L. Rubinstein, N. Alekseev, G. Kiesewalter

Lieblich

The circulated invitations proposed a visit to *Lieblich*. Before the audience's arrival (25 people), a switched-on electric bell was buried in the snow in the center of Izmailovsky Field, and it continued to ring even after the audience and participants had left the field.

April 2, 1976
Moscow, Izmailovsky Field
A. Monastyrski, N. Alekseev, G. Kiesewalter

The Tent

12 stylized paintings by N. Alekseev, each measuring a square meter, were sewn together into one large canvas, set up in the form of a tent, and left in a forest outside Moscow.

October 2, 1976
Moscow Region, Savelovskaya Railroad Line, Depot Station
N. Alekseev, M.K., A. Monastyrski, G. Kiesewalter, N. Panitkov, V. Miturich-Khlebnikova, Steffen Andre

Slogan-1977

On a hill between two trees, we hung a red banner (10 m x 1 m) with the following inscription in white letters: I DO NOT COMPLAIN ABOUT ANYTHING AND EVERYTHING PLEASES ME, DESPITE THE FACT THAT I HAVE NEVER BEEN HERE BEFORE AND KNOW NOTHING ABOUT THESE PARTS. (From the book *Nothing Happens,* by A. Monastyrski.)

January 26, 1977
Moscow Region, Leningrad Railroad Line, Firsanovka Station
A. Monastyrski, V. Miturich-Khlebnikova, N. Alekseev, G. Kiesewalter, N. Panitkov, M.K., A. Abramov

The Sphere

A spherical membrane (four meters in diameter) was sewn out of colored calico fabric. Then, in the forest, for a period of six hours, we blew up balloons in the rain to fill the calico membrane. After which, placing a switched-on electric bell inside the "sphere," we sent the resulting haystack-shaped form down the Klyazma River.

June 15, 1977
Moscow Region, Gorky Railroad Line, Nazarevo Station
A. Monastyrski, N. Alekseev, G. Kiesewalter, L. Veshnevskaya, A. Abramov, M.K.

Comedy

The invited viewers (10 people) were met at the Lobnya Station by one of the action's participants (time spent in the commuter train: 40 minutes). Taking a taxi-van to the village of Kievy Gorki (a 20-minute journey) and walking through the forest (10 minutes), the viewers came out on the edge of a field, from the opposite side of which two other action participants appeared. One of the two, significantly taller than the other, was dressed in a wide, long, light ochre colored cloak. The other, walking behind and holding the cloak's train, was dressed in regular street clothes. When there were 80 meters left between them and the audience, the cloaked participant stopped and faced the audience. The other one in the street clothes climbed under the cloak, and in this way, they both began to move in the direction of the audience. When they were 25 meters away, the participant in the cloak lifted it, and it became clear that the participant in the street clothes was no longer underneath the cloak. Then the cloaked participant turned to the right and disappeared into the forest.

October 2, 1977
Moscow Region, Savelovskaya Railroad Line, a field near the village of Kievy Gorki
A. Monastyrski, V. Miturich-Khlebnikova, N. Panitkov, N. Alekseev

The Lantern

On a hill outside the city of Zagorsk, in the twilight, we used ropes to hang an electric lantern outfitted with violet mica-clad glass between two trees. A red ball was suspended below the lantern to serve as a sail. The construction rotated and swung in the wind. Violet light flashes of different intensities and separated from each other by pauses of darkness of varying duration were visible at a distance of about two kilometers. Our field of vision contained no other sources of light except the lantern's flashes. (For several days leading up to and following November 15th, the weather was sunny and beautiful. November 15th turned out to be an unexpectedly gloomy day with wet snow.)

November 15, 1977
Moscow Region, Yaroslavskaya Railroad Line, Kalistovo Station
A. Monastyrski, N. Alekseev, I. Yavorsky, I. Pivovarova

Slogan-1978

On the bank of a river, we hung a dark-blue banner (12 m x 1 m) with the following inscription in white letters:

> STRANGE, WHY DID I LIE TO MYSELF THAT I HAVE NEVER BEEN HERE BEFORE AND KNOW NOTHING ABOUT THESE PARTS, WHEN IN REALITY, HERE IS JUST LIKE EVERYWHERE ELSE, YOU JUST FEEL IT MORE SHARPLY AND MORE DEEPLY DON'T UNDERSTAND.

April 9, 1978
Moscow Region, Belorusskaya Railroad Line, near the city of Zvenigorod
A. Monastyrski, N. Alekseev, I. Yavorsky, V. and L. Veshnevsky, G. Kiesewalter

The Third Variant

The invited viewers (around 20 people) were situated on the edge of a field. From the forest to the right, at a distance of 50 meters from the viewers, a participant in a violet cloak appeared, walked a certain distance along the field (parallel to the line of viewers) and lay down in a ditch so that he was no longer visible. After three minutes, from another ditch dug 30 meters to the left of the place where the first participant had disappeared, there appeared a figure in an identical violet cloak but with a red balloon in place of a head. Piercing the balloon with a stick and creating a cloud of white dust, the participant—now headless—once again lay down in the ditch from which he had just appeared. Concurrent with this disappearance, the participant appeared again from the first hole (30 meters to the right), but now he wore regular street clothes and, after filling the ditch from which he had just emerged with earth, withdrew into the forest in the same direction from which he had come at the beginning of the action.

May 28, 1978
Moscow Region, Savelovskaya Railroad Line, a field near the village of Kievy Gorki
A. Monastyrski, V. Miturich-Khlebnikova, N. Panitkov, N. Alekseev, M.K.

Time of Action

In a forest, not far from the edge of a field, among the trees, we hung a drum on which we had previously wound seven kilometers of white string. The drum was hung in such a way that it was not visible from the opposite side of the field, where, across 200 meters of open space and freshly plowed earth, the end of the string was drawn and the audience (20 people) and two action participants were located. Meanwhile, the third participant was standing in the forest by the drum.

From 1:30 until 3:00 (1.5 hours) in the afternoon, the action participants and some audience members took turns continuously pulling the rope that was unwinding from the drum. The rope's end was not attached to the drum, and in this way, all of the rope was pulled out of the forest in the course of the action.

October 15, 1978
Moscow Region, Savelovskaya Railroad Line, a field near the village of Kievy Gorki
A. Monastyrski, N. Alekseev, N. Panitkov, A. Abramov (photo)

Pictures

The organizers made 104 envelopes out of white and colored paper of various sizes. (The largest envelope was 40 x 42 cm; the smallest was 13 x 8 cm.) These were inserted one into the other to make 12 sets, each containing 12 envelopes. Written on each envelope was a description possessing a formal relationship to moments of the event in accordance with the following 12 paradigms: (1) Instructions to the audience; (2) The time of action for the entire action; (3) The place of action; (4) The weather; (5) The color of the envelopes; (6) The sound; (7) The object of perception; (8) The time of the gesture's (action's) conclusion; (9) The audience reaction; (10) The meaning of the gesture (action); (11) The interpretation, indication; (12) Factography. These sets were distributed on the field to members of the invited audience (30 people, 12 of whom received sets). While the viewers were opening the envelopes and arranging them in a line (of roughly 50 meters) on the snow before themselves, three participants, who had separated from the viewers, crossed the field and disappeared into the forest. After reading the inscriptions on all of the envelopes in the line, the viewers assembled and glued each set of envelopes together in such away as to make 12 multi-colored pictures, or "frames," with the largest envelope at the base, then the next largest one, and so on. All of the inscriptions, except for the factographic text (that is, the indication of the place of action, the time of action, and the list of the organizers' names), were hidden by the envelopes glued over them. These pictures were then distributed to the audience as the factographic document of the action.

February 11, 1979
Moscow Region, Paveletskaya Railroad Line, Rastorguevo Station, Sukhanovo Park
A. Monastyrski, N. Alekseev, N. Panitkov, I. Yavorsky

1. The Shoot

The invited audience (30 people) were brought to the edge of a field and invited to have their pictures taken for a slide-film while moving along a straight line through the field in the direction of the opposite the forest (350 meters away). The line of the journey was marked out ahead of time with 15 small round cardboard circles laid on the ground, each inscribed with the number of the shooting position (with position one being the closest and position 15 the farthest from the initial shooting position). These positions divided the line of the journey into equal sections of approximately 23 meters. Arriving at each position, the viewers were supposed to turn and face the initial position (i.e., toward the shooting camera) and, after pausing for five seconds, continue moving to the next position. Each viewer's shoot began once the previous viewer disappeared into the forest on the opposite side of the field. After the shoot of 15 viewers was conducted in this way, additional shoots were carried out (partly on that day, and partly on October 13, 1979).

2. The Curtain

Before the start of the shoot, between the thirteenth and fourteenth positions (that is, at a distance of 300 meters from the initial shooting position), we set up a curtain made of violet fabric (3 x 2 m), which was initially gathered to the left side when the first viewer approached. The viewers were advised that, when they reach the curtain, they should unfold it in such a way that the curtain would divide them from the group of people at the initial shooting position, that is, so that the viewer would end up on the other side of the curtain. On the back side of the curtain was a message inviting the viewer to replace the previous viewer who was lying in a ditch. (We dug the ditch ahead of time at the fourteenth shooting position, and one of the action participants was lying in it and holding a camera prior to the first viewer's arrival at the ditch.) In this way, hidden by the curtain from the group of viewers at the starting position, the viewer replaced the previous viewer lying in the ditch, and the person who was replaced returned to the curtain and moved it back over to the left. (The message on the curtain gave the instructions for this as well.) Then finally, this viewer, who had previously been lying in the ditch, photographed the viewer who had replaced him in the ditch, left him the camera, and continued on to be photographed at the remaining two positions (i.e., the 14th and 15th).

Having been shot at each position along the line and thus having carried out the "curtain" action, the viewers, one after another, passed into the forest, where a placard (130 x 90 cm) was installed on a tree, containing a schematic plan illustrating the audience shoot, a plan of the additional participant shoot, and also the subsequent parts of the slide-film and collection of images for a black-and-white exposition that it was suggested might be compiled based on the materials of the completed shoots. Next to the placard stood another participant holding a tape-recorder and recording the observations of the viewers who had taken part in the action.

Moscow Region, Savelovskaya Railroad Line, a field near the village of Kievy Gorki
October 7, 1979

3. The Slide-Film

Based on the materials collected during the shoots, a slide-film and a black-and-white exposition were assembled. After the demonstration of the slide-film, a tape-recorded commentary to it was played. Then, additional documentation in the form of slides was shown, accompanied by the tape recording made at the placard on October 7th.

October 31, 1979
Moscow
A. Monastyrski, I. Makarevich, N. Alekseev, N. Panitkov, E. Elagina

For N. Panitkov (Three Darknesses)

A Note on the Descriptive Text (Plan of Action)

1. Not knowing the details of the action, Panitkov and V.D. arrive at a snowy clearing in the forest in daytime. A small hole is dug in the

snow and a chair is placed inside. Panitkov sits in the chair, and the remaining participants, covering the sitting Panitkov with a placard (using vertical stakes installed in the snow at the corners of the ditch), begin to pour snow onto the placard to make a hill containing Panitkov in darkness.

The participants arrange ahead of time with Panitkov that he should stand up from the chair and lift the placard above his head once it gets quiet for the second time. (During the entire action, six radios were turned up to full volume and set on different frequencies all around and near Panitkov's hill.)

2. After building Panitkov's hill, another hill is built next to it in which sits V.D. (Panitkov does not know about this second hill, because the sound of the work accompanying the preparation of the second hill is drowned out by the radios).

The participants arrange with V.D. ahead of time that he should stand from the chair and lift the placard above his head once it gets quiet for the first time.

3. After V.D.'s hill is constructed, Panitkov's hill is covered with black light-impermeable fabric no smaller in size than 4 m x 4 m.

4. Using ropes attached to trees and black light-impermeable paper or fabric, a box is built above the two snow hills, five meters in length, four meters in width, and two and a half meters in height.

5. After the light-impermeable box is built, a participant holding a camera with a flash enters inside.
All of the radios are turned off.
V.D. stands up inside his hill and lifts the placard above his head.
At this moment, the participant with the camera takes several shots and then both of them exit the box after destroying the snowy remains of V.D.'s hill.
The radios are once again turned on.

6. Three or four minutes after the two participants exit the box, the radios are turned off for a second time.

7. Panitkov, sitting all the while in the darkness inside his hill (the first darkness of the hill), stands up from his chair and lifts the placard above his head.
8. Breaking open his hill in this way, he remains in the darkness (the second darkness of the fabric), since his hill is covered by a light-impermeable fabric.
9. Pulling this fabric from himself, Panitkov continues to remain in the darkness (the third darkness of the box).
10. Panitkov's further actions are undertaken at his own discretion.

Descriptive Text

The plan of action in the form that it had been conceived was not realized. Only Panitkov's hill was built, and the darkness of the fabric did not take place, because the fabric turned out too small and was thrown off by Panitkov along with the placard. The darkness of the box turned out (due to tiny holes in the paper) to be somewhat brighter than the darkness of the hill.

February 17, 1980
Moscow Region, Rizhskaya Railroad Line, Snegiri Station
A. Monastyrski, N. Alekseev, E. Elagina, S. Romashko, I. Makarevich, I. Yavorsky

For A. Monastyrski

Seven action participants lined up at a distance of 15 paces from each other facing the viewer (A. Monastyrski) on an untrampled snowy field bordered on one side by a forest. A. Monastyrski was located across from the fourth participant at a distance of 20 paces.

Just before the start of the action, Monastyrski was given a tape recorder and oral instructions to turn the tape recorder to play at the command of one of the participants. Further instructions regarding the participants' and Monastyrski's actions had been recorded on the tape.

The commands were given to each participant sequentially at small intervals, so that the movement of several participants took place simultaneously. That is, from Monastyrski's perspective, there was a picture of continuous movement from the entire group of participants according to some particular plan, but one that was not intelligible to him.

10 minutes after the start of the action came the first command for Monastyrski, which invited him to move from the "zone of observation" to a predetermined position located on the line where the participants had originally been stationed. In this way, the prescribed temporal distance (10 minutes) between the start of the participants' movements and the start of Monastyrski's movement was preserved for the duration of the entire action and made evident at the end of the action, when each participant, having gone through his or her route, had already disappeared into the forest and Monastyrski still continued to move for 10 more minutes in the field following the instructions recorded on the tape. (Accordingly, the temporal intervals between the commands, now meant for Monastyrski alone, were increased.)

Movement through the field was accompanied by significant physical effort, since the depth of the snow had reached 50–60 cm.

The participants' tracks, which should have fairly clearly reproduced in the snow the "general schema of movement," naturally changed its design.

The action lasted 30 minutes.

March 16, 1980
Paveletskaya Railroad Line, Rastorguevo Station
N. Panitkov, N. Alekseev, E. Elagina, I. Makarevich, V.D., S. Romashko, I. Yavorsky

For G. Kiesewalter (Slogan-1980)

IN THE SPRING, ON THE EDGE OF A FIELD, IN THE TREES, G. KIESEWALTER HUNG A WHITE BANNER (950 x 80 CM) WITH AN INSCRIPTION IN WHITE LETTERS.

April 13, 1980
Yakutskaya ASSR, near the city of Mirnyi
A. Monastyrski, N. Alekseev, E. Elagina, N. Panitkov, V.D., S. Romashko, I. Yavorsky, I. Makarevich

Ten Appearances

10 participants, together with the organizers, arrived at the action in the middle of a large snow-covered field surrounded by forest, knowing neither its title, nor what was to take place.

On a board (60 x 90 cm) laid on the snow, using vertically-driven nails, ten spools holding anywhere from 200 to 300 meters of strong white string were secured around the board's perimeter. Each participant was invited to take one string and, unwinding it from the spool, to move in a straight line away from the board, so that together, the participants would move in radiating lines out toward the surrounding forest. This movement was begun by each participant simultaneously on the organizers' command.

The participants were to move in straight lines in the direction of the forest and then, entering the forest, to continue in the same direction into its interior for approximately 50 to 100 meters more, to points from which the field could no longer be seen.

Each participant's path was thus meant to constitute a distance of 300 to 400 meters, and moreover, movement through the field and in the forest required significant physical effort, since the snow was between 50 and 100 centimeters deep. Having finished the route, each participant (still following the initial instructions) was to retrieve the other end of the string (which was not secured to the spool) to which was tied a slip of paper with a factographic text: the organizers' names and the action's time and location.

Since no additional instructions were given, the participants, having retrieved the factographic text, had to determine all further actions on their own, i.e. either to return to the center of the field where the organizers were located, or not to return, to leave the place of action, and to continue moving through the forest.

Eight participants returned to the center of the field within an hour (I. Pivovarova, N. Kozlov, V. Skersis, L. Talochkin, O. Vassiliev, I. Kabakov, I. Chuikov, Yu. Albert). Seven of them returned along their own paths, while one (N. Kozlov) came back along a neighboring path. Two participants—V. Nekrasov and A. Zhigalov—did not return.

The returning participants each received a photograph (30 x 40 cm) glued to a piece of cardboard containing an image of that section of the forest toward which the participant receiving the photograph had walked at the start of the action. Each photograph showed the barely discernible figure of a person appearing from the forest and was furnished with a label-signature indicating the names of the action's authors, its title—*Ten Appearances*—and the event represented in the photograph (i.e. the "appearance" of the participant to whom it was given; for example: "The appearance of I. Chuikov on the first of February, 1981"). These photographs were prepared a week prior to the realization of the action: the organizers of the action were photographed in the "line of indistinguishability" in the same directions that the participants were told to move during the action and from which they then appeared.

February 1, 1981
Moscow Region, Savelovskaya Railroad Line, Kievy Gorki
A. Monastyrski, G. Kiesewalter, S. Romashko, N. Alekseev, I. Makarevich, E. Elagina

Playback

The action took place in N. Alekseev's apartment. The invited viewers were seated facing an empty light-gray wall next to which, to the right and left, two small cassette-tape players stood atop speaker units. The tape players were switched on, and for a period of 10 minutes, the sounds of banging and knocking on the wall were heard. Upon careful inspection, two marks (indentations) could be discovered above the tape players made by hammer blows to the wall during the recording of the banging. (The recording had been produced on the eve of the action.) When these two soundtracks concluded, a third, stereophonic tape player was switched on. (It had been positioned at the back wall and covered with a cloth to keep from drawing the viewers' notice.) It was connected to the speakers on which the cassette-tape players were located. Its soundtrack consisted of a recording of the arrival and seating of the viewers—knocks at the door, noises, conversations (produced during the 15 minutes prior to the cassette-tape players' being switched on)—and a recording of the sounds of the two cassette-tape players as they were heard by the audience.

March 1, 1981
Moscow
A. Monastyrski, S. Romashko, N. Panitkov, N. Alekseev, G. Kiesewalter, I. Makarevich, E. Elagina

MOST OF THE ACTIONS described here consist of a situation in which a group of people is invited by the action's organizers to participate in an activity that is unknown to them. Everything that takes place in such a situation can be divided into that which takes place in the empirical sphere (according to the organizers' preliminary plan) and that which takes place in the sphere of the psychological, that is, the experience of the events in the participants' field of vision during the action and the experience of that which precedes and accompanies action.

Since in our work we are particularly interested in the realm of the psychological, the "interior," we are obliged to pay special attention to all kinds of preliminary events, to that which takes place as though "on the edges" of the action's demonstrational "field." The demonstrational field itself expands and becomes the object of observation: on it, we try to discover zones that possess certain properties and interrelationships. These properties and relationships, as we imagine them, act to produce different levels of perception, on one of which can be attained an experience of the events as events taking place essentially "inside" a liberating consciousness. Such is the overall goal of the actions. In a constructive sense, the goal consists of keeping from artificially breaching the boundaries of direct perception within which nearly every action begins its unfolding.

In this respect, our approach to the plots of the actions naturally changes. The mythological or symbolic content of the plot is not significant (according to the organizers' conception) relative to the construction of that level of perception for which the plot, as one of the constructive elements, serves as an instrument.

Still, any activity on the demonstrational field, however minimal, prompts interpretation, and on the metaphorical layer of the demonstrational field itself is laid another layer: the viewer begins to wonder about the meaning of this or that action and finally "discovers" its mythological or some other kind of content. It is true that the structure of some actions is such that they contain the interpretive process within themselves ("interpretationality" as such). That is, in the course of their realization, the necessity to "interpret through," as a psychological necessity, is embodied in the form of a specifi-cally directed—and for the organizers, invariably false—understanding. In this way, an expanded interpretation is precluded during the action, though later, it is unavoidable, and since the actions are usually fairly brief, the participants may experience the sense that they discerned this "mythologic-ity" during action itself. For us, the problem of free interpretation is funda-mentally important. We regard free interpretation as the demonstrational position of the "outside observer." This is the sole position, for example, occupied by the reader of the actions' descriptive texts. There are, however, certain means by which the formation of this position is forestalled during the action itself and, in large part, for some time after its visible conclu-sion. One such method is the introduction of an extra-demonstrational ele-ment, whose action prolongs the level of experience and creates a sense of indeterminacy in the action's temporal conclusion. The introduction of the extra-demonstrational element into the demonstrational structure at vari-ous points during action, and its course at the time of the demonstration will hence on be called "empty action."

In order for the viewers to realize that their consciousness was involved in the construction of the event (or in the preparation for the act of self-awareness), and—as becomes clear in recollection—in order for them to understand the fact that during the preceding, their consciousness was in fact the object of the demonstration for a physically nonexistant "outside observer," we introduce "empty action." Signifying the system of demonstrational relations, empty action shapes the the viewer-participants' consciousness as yet another one of the components of the aesthetic act.

Here we have defined "empty action" as a principle, though in each action, it expresses itself in its own way, and is regarded as the specific temporal section of the action when the audience, if it can be expressed this way, "intensely does not understand" or "incorrectly understands" what is taking place. Leaping ahead, we should note that those acts or events by means of which "empty action" is realized (appearance, disappearance, withdrawal, doubling, etc.) not only create the conditions for meditation on the level of direct perception, but also become its focus.

We consider the relationship between objecthood and subjecthood in their reciprocal relation to be an extremely important element of the demonstrational structure. The reader will have no difficulty noticing that the movement of figures and objects in the described actions occurs for the most part along a straight line in two directions: either away from the viewers or toward the viewers. In the given context, this movement should be understood as a movement along a kind of "line of perception," which appears as an accessory of the demonstrational model.

And so, all of the figures and stages of the action are like the "traces of a pencil" sketching out the edges, zones, and relations of the empty (pure) demonstrational "field," through which the participants and organizers "pass" in the course of the action's realization. Here we would like to pause briefly on the notion of the demonstrational field itself and to try in general terms to describe certain of its stages, conditions, and structures, taking into account and partly proceeding from the impressions of the participants.

The initial experience of the viewer-participant who is invited to an action can be defined as a state of anticipation. Prior to the start of the event in the empirical field, this "field" of anticipation becomes filled with all sorts of presentiments and presuppositions. Obviously, the more "unknown" the event promised in the invitation, the less concrete these presentiments and presuppositions are. The tendency of this experience is such that if this concreteness is reduced to a minimum, then the field of anticipation will remain practically empty and in a heightened state of tension until the very start of action. Here a large role is played by the different contexts that together form a particular historico-contextual background that must be kept in mind in planning the action. The goal is, on the one hand, for the action to relate to this background, while on the other, for the action to surpass its borders and thereby to change the overall contextual background. (In this sense, the diffusion of certain elements and, more importantly, principles of various spiritual practices into contemporary aesthetics seems to us significant and decisive.)

And so, if the field of anticipation is "empty," then anticipation itself as a psychological experience becomes concentrated and is sensed as a nearly sufficient (pre-sufficient) state. There appears the impression that action has already begun, while in reality the one experiencing this condition has not yet reached the point from where action can be seen (or heard).

We used two different means to create this preliminary impression, which can be called pre-anticipation. The first is the form of the invitation (or preliminary instruction), and the second is the particular spatio-temporal features of the journey to the place of action. With regard to the further unfolding of the demonstrational field, we shall call the field of pre-anticipation that psychological field which has not yet been "linked up" via the visual field with the real (empirical) field on which one expects to "see" some anticipated event.

Here we can give a preliminary definition of the demonstrational field as the totality of the psychological, visual, and empirical fields. It includes, it is important to note, both the experiences and events preceding action itself as well as those continuing after its conclusion.

The indistinct spatio-temporal boundaries of pre-anticipation become concentrated into the more rigid spatial and temporal constraints of anticipation proper at the moment of the viewer-participants' exit from the forest onto the empty open field on the simplest of instructions or notifications of the sort: "Here is where it will take place." It is necessary to consider in more detail this actual field, which in such a psychological situation surely and subconsciously becomes endowed with the epithet "empty." The actual field may be brown, green, level, humped, etc., but it is perfectly clear that in this moment, its main feature, for the person who has experienced pre-anticipation and is now experiencing anticipation, is its "emptiness."

The experience of this "emptiness" of the actual field and the continuing experience of anticipation as an empty "field of anticipation" become linked up. The real field becomes metaphorized and may at a certain point be perceived as an extension of the field of anticipation, taking on qualities inherent to psychological fields, such as "invisibility," non-objectivity, or "interiority," in other words, properties not contraposed to consciousness. We should note that it is precisely the vast free space of a fairly large actual field—when the visual field seems to freely unfold in space and the field of anticipation "unfolds" with it—that gives the effect of maintaining concentrated anticipation for a protracted length of time.

Here arises the problem of not upsetting this state with the crude incursion of some object or event into the visual field. As we already said above, we do not have the goal of "showing" something to the viewer-participants. The goal consists of preserving the impression of anticipation as of an important, significant event. However, if pre-anticipation demands its resolution in anticipation, which is what is accomplished, then anticipation, in turn, also demands its own resolution in some new experience; in other words, it necessarily demands the start of action—otherwise it cannot realize itself as its own object. Having preserved the liberation of consciousness from the direct sphere of everyday perception, which is achieved through its being "conducted" as though along the periphery of the demonstrational field, it is important at this point that the planned event of the action itself act upon that consciousness in such a way as to keep it from returning to that initial state preceding pre-anticipation, and that it is preserved within its proper self, in its own liberation, as it enters the phase of the perception of entirely real events.

To do this, we make use of the device of gradually bringing the object of perception (the figures of the participant-organizers) out of invisibility, through the zone of indistinguishability, and into the zone of distinguishability on the empirical plane of the demonstrational field. (Here we refer to a particular group of actions: *Appearance, Comedy, The Third Variant, Pictures,* and *Place of Action.*)

And yet, if up to this point we had the experience of pure anticipation, then now, with the appearance of the object of perception in the real field, this experience ceases, breaks off, and there begins the process of intensified looking, and moreover, there appears the desire to understand the meaning of this object. From our point of view, this new stage of perception is a pause, a necessary step in the process of perception, but in no way is it the event for the sake of which everything had been devised. We should say straightaway that the events of the action itself are undertaken in order to "distract the eyes." The nature of anticipation demands that this step is carried out, and to avoid it in the context of the given problem is impossible. But it is possible to "deceive" perception, that is, to complete this step but then to let the audience know that "while everyone was looking in one direction, the main event was taking place in a completely different place," in this case in the consciousnesses of the viewers themselves.

There is one important point here that must be clarified, specifically, that the event was taking place. That is, by the time it is understood that the "looking" was a "looking in the wrong direction," the main event has already happened. In the present moment, it can only be remembered, but to observe it consciously is impossible, since during the time when it takes its course, consciousness is occupied elsewhere, is directed toward the perception of something else.

But what was it that actually took place? If what took place in the actual field was false, then in relation to what truth should this falseness be understood? What does it indicate? Evidently, at this point in the demonstration, we are "surrounded" by a fairly large "field" of anticipation; we seem to have delved fairly deeply into it and away from its edges, and have now closed in upon ourselves, since what was being demonstrated to us was in reality a demonstration of our own perception and nothing more. It is this pure anticipation that was the thing that took place in reality, and what is more, it was anticipation that was completed. What was completed, what took place, was not what we expected, not some concrete event contraposed to us, but it was precisely anticipation itself that took place and was completed. In other words, the pause that was the perception of the object concluded with the same anticipation, but now taking place on another level of perception and not perceived as such during its passage: it was experienced in recollection at a certain point in the action. After this point, the conclusion of action (the figure's departure from the field) is perceived with complete immediacy, seemingly outside its own conventionality, on the same level as the trees, the grass, the viewers themselves; in other words, it has been de-metaphorized.

It is important to understand that the actual "field of action" again becomes an "empty" field even before the participant-organizer has left it. As a result of certain acts by the participant-organizers, this field is once again metaphorized as "empty": there appears a place or a level of a kind of "heightened emptiness," with which the recollecting (understanding) consciousness of the participant-viewers enters into metaphorical contact, while the participant-organizer seems to "slip off" after this point of action onto the empirical field. In other words, while still located in the empirical zone of the demonstrational field, the participant-organizer ceases to be the object of the demonstration within the action structure and becomes simply a person who is exiting and exits into the forest, just as at the start, he was simply a person appearing in the distance out of the forest.

We should clarify that in this preface we are considering only one, superficial, part of the entire situation, the part "for the viewers," more or less related to aesthetic problems. Its inner meaning—related to the main goal of the action, specifically, the attainment of a particular spiritual experience, which is in its essence not symbolic, and which has real significance exclusively for the organizers acting in the field—is not considered.

And so, in order to create this type of situation, none of the objects and figures of movement (which for us, as we said above, usually form a straight line from the object of perception to the subject or vice-versa, that is, movement along the "line" of a subjective-objective relation) used in action should have independent meaning; they "should not have anything written on them" apart from the figures of the participants having a significance specifically and solely as "participants" in relation to the "viewers." And if some object is used, then it should be used exclusively to generate some specific condition of perception, for example, to create invisibility, an impression of likeness, and so forth.

As we said above, the appearance of the object of perception in our actions takes place out of invisibility and through indistinguishability, which demands a familiar adaptation of the perceiver's vision. This device allows for the coordination of the psychological and the empirical zones of the demonstrational field.

And so, following the appearance of the figure, there unfolds some "false" event in the zone of "distinguishability," and then at last, the proceedings divide sharply into (1) the empirical event, brought out into the realm of immediacy after the moment of the viewers' understanding that action was false or "empty"; and (2) the psychological event—the experience of completed anticipation.

At the moment of this division, it is as if consciousness casts off the concreteness of its anticipation. That is, anticipation that is completed in recollection is anticipation that is removed in its concreteness. Consequently, memory in this situation likewise becomes a psychological zone of the demonstrational field. This moment can be described in the following way. The reality of action was concluded at the moment when the object of perception emerged from the zone of indistinguishability into the zone of indirect, contraposed perception. The operations of the participant-organizers in the zone of distinguishability were undertaken in order to leave the authenticity of action in the past, to keep from bringing it into the present: "it concluded then," not "it concluded now." But we discovered it only now. In the gap between "then" and "now," we were lying to ourselves, but only in the moment of "now" were we told about this. This temporal gap between "then" and "now" is the distance (in our memory) between our anticipation and us. We "gaze" at it from here, in a state of "undeception," we are freed from self-deception in one of its concrete, temporal expressions-manifestations. To "gaze" at anticipation is in reality to experience anticipation as an anticipation of completed liberation from one's own self. It is likely that the strangeness of this experience in the context of the demonstration (though it may not even be understood in the way that it is described here, and should not even be understood in this way) is what gives rise to the feeling of a promise fulfilled, that we were "not deceived."

In a strictly aesthetic sense, the actions presented here could be characterized as attempts to make strange the perception of ordinary appearance, disappearance, recession, light, sound, etc.

A. Monastyrski
June 1980

Bibliographical Note

COLLECTIVE ACTIONS' documentary materials were originally compiled into self-published volumes called *Trips out of Town*, which appeared in a limited number of hand-bound, typed copies beginning in 1980. The audience recollections translated here are taken from the first two volumes of *Trips out of Town*, *Poezdki za gorod* (1980) and *Poezdki i vosproizvedenie* (1983). The authors of the first volume of *Trips out of Town* were Nikita Alekseev, George Kiesewalter, Andrei Monastyrski, and Nikolai Panitkov. By the time the second volume was compiled, the group had added three new members, Igor Makarevich, Sergei Romashko, and Elena Elagina. (Collective Actions' eighth member, Sabine Hänsgen, joined the group during the period of actions compiled in the third volume, which came out in 1985.) The book form of *Trips out of Town* was first published in 1998, by Ad Marginem in Moscow. This volume, also titled *Poezdki za gorod* and published under the collective authorship of Kollektivnye deistviia (Collective Actions), chronicled the group's activities from 1976 through 1989 and thus contained the first five volumes of *Trips out of Town*. Beginning in 2009, German Titov's Vologda imprint Biblioteka Moskovskogo Kontseptualizma began to release new editions of *Trips out of Town*, publishing the combined Volumes 6–11 in 2009, and expanded versions of Volumes 1 and 2–3 in 2011, including previously unpublished texts and photographs. In addition to this, much of Collective Actions' documentary and theoretical material (in Russian and in various translations) can be found online on two different web portals devoted to the school of Moscow Conceptualism. These are http://conceptualism.letov.ru and http://www.conceptualism-moscow.org. What follows is a list of transliterated titles of the texts included in the present book. The Russian originals of these texts can be found in the various aforementioned incarnations of the first two volumes of *Trips out of Town* (abbreviated below as *Pzg* 1 and *Pzg* 2).

Irina Pivovarova, "Rasskaz I. Pivovarovoi ob aktsiiakh 'Liblikh', 'Fonar'', 'Vremia deistviia'" (November 1980), *Pzg* 1.

Ilya Kabakov, "Rasskaz I. Kabakova ob aktsiiakh 'Komediia', 'Tretii variant', 'Kartiny'" (April 1980), *Pzg* 1.

Ivan Chuikov, "Rasskaz I. Chuikova ob aktsiiakh 'Vremia deistviia', 'Kartiny'" (July 1980), *Pzg* 1.

Ilya Kabakov, "Rasskaz I. Kabakova ob aktsii 'Mesto deistviia'" (November 1980), *Pzg* 1.

Vladimir Mironenko, "Rasskaz V. Mironenko ob aktsii 'Mesto deistviia'" (June 1980), *Pzg* 1.

George Kiesewalter, "Rasskaz G. Kizeval'tera ob aktsii 'G. Kizeval'teru'" (April 3, 1980), *Pzg* 1.

Ilya Kabakov, "Rasskaz I. Kabakova (Ob aktsii 'Desiat' poiavlenii')" (February 8, 1981), *Pzg* 2.

Vsevolod Nekrasov, "Rasskaz V. Nekrasova (Ob aktsii 'Desiat' poiavlenii')" (February 1981), *Pzg* 2.

List of Authors and Group Members

NIKITA ALEKSEEV (b. 1953), artist, founding member of Collective Actions, and founder of the AptArt Gallery in 1982.

IVAN CHUIKOV (b. 1935), painter and regular audience member of Collective Actions' performances.

ELENA ELAGINA (b. 1949), artist and member of Collective Actions since 1979. Frequent collaborator with spouse, Igor Makarevich.

ILYA KABAKOV (b. 1933), artist and regular member of Collective Actions' performances.

GEORGE KIESEWALTER (b. 1953), artist and founding member of Collective Actions.

IGOR MAKAREVICH (b. 1943), artist and member of Collective Actions since 1979. Frequent collaborator with spouse, Elena Elagina.

VLADIMIR MIRONENKO (b. 1959), artist and member of the Mukhomor (Toadstool) Group.

ANDREI MONASTYRSKI (b. 1949), poet and founding member of Collective Actions.

VSEVOLOD NEKRASOV (1934–2009), poet and regular audience member of Collective Actions' performances.

NIKOLAI PANITKOV (b. 1952), artist, collector, and member of Collective Actions.

IRINA PIVOVAROVA (1939–1986), author and illustrator of children's books and regular audience member of Collective Actions' performances.

SERGEI ROMASHKO (b. 1952), philologist, artist, and member of Collective Actions.

List of Illustrations

Photographs by:
Andrei Abramov
Igor Makarevich
George Kiesewalter
Nikita Alekseev
Elena Elagina

Frontispiece: *Appearance,* March 13, 1976. The audience waiting in the field.

1.   *Appearance,* March 13, 1976. Two organizers in the distance.
2.   *Appearance,* March 13, 1976. Documentary certificate.
3.   *Place of Action,* October 31, 1979. Slide-film and post-action discussion in Makarevich's studio. (Photo courtesy of Igor Makarevich.)
4.   *Place of Action,* October 7, 1979. One stopping point in the field.
5.   *Place of Action,* October 7, 1979. The signboard in the forest.
6.   *Appearance,* March 13, 1976. The audience waiting in the field.
7.   *Ten Appearances,* February 1, 1981. Factographic document illustrating "The Appearance of V. Nekrasov."
8–12.   *Lieblich,* April 2, 1976. The audience in the field.
13–16. *The Lantern,* November 15, 1977. The flickering lantern light.
17.   *Time of Action,* October 15, 1978. The audience in the field.
18.   *Time of Action,* October 15, 1978. The stretched rope.
19.   *Time of Action,* October 15, 1978. Andrei Monastyrski pulling the rope.
20.   *Time of Action,* October 15, 1978. Andrei Monastyrski and Nikita Alekseev pulling the rope.
21.   *Time of Action,* October 15, 1978. Nikolai Panitkov with Nikita Alekseev and Andrei Monastyrski in the forest.
22.   *Time of Action,* October 15, 1978. The pile of rope.
23–24. *Comedy,* October 2, 1977. The figures' action in the field.
25.   *Comedy,* October 2, 1977. The figure exiting the field.

61.   *Place of Action,* October 7, 1979. Signboard with action documentation at the conclusion of the action.

62.   *Place of Action,* October 7, 1979. Participants at the beginning of the action holding instruction sheets.

63.   *Place of Action,* October 7, 1979. Vladimir Mironenko lying in the ditch.

64.   *Place of Action,* October 7, 1979. Group of participants.

65–72. *Place of Action,* October 7, 1979. Participants at the curtain.

73.   *Place of Action,* October 7, 1979. The curtain.

74.   *For G. Kiesewalter,* April 13, 1980. The tree with the metal stakes in the trunk.

75.   *For G. Kiesewalter,* April 13, 1980. The sign, as it arrived in the mail.

76.   *For G. Kiesewalter,* April 13, 1980. The sign, ready to be hung.

77.   *For G. Kiesewalter,* April 13, 1980. The hanging sign with the corner of the slogan uncovered.

78.   *For G. Kiesewalter,* April 13, 1980. The hanging sign with the slogan uncovered, photographed from a distance.

79.   *Ten Appearances,* February 1, 1981. The participants gathered around the board at beginning of action.

80.   *Ten Appearances,* February 1, 1981. Andrei Monastyrski and others at the board with bobbins of string.

81.   *Ten Appearances,* February 1, 1981. The participants following faintly marked dashes in different directions toward the forest.

82.   *Ten Appearances,* February 1, 1981. The participants in the field.

83.   *Ten Appearances,* February 1, 1981. The participants holding documentary certificates at the completion of the action.

84.   *Ten Appearances,* February 1, 1981. The participants following faintly marked dashes in different directions toward the forest.

85.   *Ten Appearances,* February 1, 1981. A participant heading toward the forest.

86.   *Ten Appearances,* February 1, 1981. Tracks in the snow.

87.   *Ten Appearances,* February 1, 1981. A participant returning from the forest.

88.   *Ten Appearances,* February 1, 1981. Tracks in the snow and participants in the field.

89.   *Ten Appearances,* February 1, 1981. A participant returning from the forest.

90–91. *Ten Appearances,* February 1, 1981. Tracks in the snow and participant in the field.

92.   *Ten Appearances,* February 1, 1981. Tracks in the snow.

93.   *Ten Appearances,* February 1, 1981. Factographic document illustrating "The Appearance of V. Nekrasov."